Karl Elze, Samuel Rowley

When you See me, you Know me

A Chronicle-History

Karl Elze, Samuel Rowley

When you See me, you Know me
A Chronicle-History

ISBN/EAN: 9783337729554

Printed in Europe, USA, Canada, Australia, Japan

Cover: Foto ©ninafisch / pixelio.de

More available books at **www.hansebooks.com**

WHEN YOU SEE ME, YOU KNOW ME.

WHEN YOU SEE ME, YOU KNOW ME.

A CHRONICLE-HISTORY BY

SAMUEL ROWLEY.

EDITED

WITH AN INTRODUCTION AND NOTES

BY

KARL ELZE,
PH. D. HON. M. R. S. L.

DESSAU:
EMIL BARTH,
1874.
LONDON: WILLIAMS AND NORGATE.

INTRODUCTION.

SAMUEL ROWLEY shares the fate of many minor poets of the Elizabethan age, of whose lives no record has reached us. We know nothing of him except that he was 'Servant to the Prince', i. e. Prince Henry, and that he probably died between 1632 and 1634. The former fact he states himself on the title of his Chronicle-History '*When you see me, you know me*', while the latter circumstance, overlooked hitherto by the bibliographers, is to be collected from the Publisher's preface to his tragedy of '*The Noble Soldier*' (1634), where this play is termed a '*Posthumus*'.[1] The last quarto of '*When you see me, you know me*' (1632) has no publisher's or printer's preface, which was usual only in posthumous publications, and was therefore most probably published in the life-time of the author. Besides these two printed plays of Samuel Rowley Mr. Halliwell in his Dictionary of Old English Plays enumerates six manuscript ones, the titles of which are almost all taken from Sir Henry Herbert's manuscript diary. They are:

1. *Judas*, written by Samuel Rowley and William Borne and acted in 1601.

2. *Sampson*, a play, by Edward Jubye, assisted by Samuel Rowley. Acted in 1602.

3. *Joshua*, acted by the Lord Admiral's Servants, 1602. 'Not now known', adds Mr. Halliwell.

4. *Hymen's Holiday;* or, *Cupid's Fagaries* [sic!], acted at Court in 1612, and revived with some alterations, before the king and queen at Whitehall, 1633.

---

[1] Although on the title of *The Noble Soldier* the author's name is only indicated by the initials S. R., yet by tradition and common consent it is ascribed to Samuel Rowley.

5. *Richard the Third*, thus alluded to by Sir Henry Herbert under the date of July 27th, 1623, — 'for the Palsgrave's players, a tragedy of Richard the Third, or the English Profit, with the Reformation, written by Samuel Rowley'.

6. *Hard Shift for Husbands*, mentioned by Sir Henry under the date of October 29th, 1623, in the following words: 'for the Palsgrave's players, a new comedy called *Hard Shifte for Husbands*, or *Bilboes the Best Blade*, written by Samuel Rowley. [1]

It would hardly be worth while to search for these manuscripts, since the two printed plays raise no great appetite for more. In a dramatic and poetical point of view they are of very indifferent value and the Chronicle History '*When you see me, you know me*' is the only one which may lay claim to literary interest and consequence, having in all probability served Shakespeare as an inducement to dramatize the life of Henry VIII., a subject which at the end of the sixteenth and in the beginning of the seventeenth century seems to have been highly popular with the dramatists of the age. We know from Henslowe's Diary that in 1601 and 1602 'The Rising of Cardinal Wolsey' by Munday, Drayton, Chettle, and Wentworth Smith and Chettle's 'Cardinal Wolsey' were on the stage, and Shakespeare's K. Henry VIII. was most likely written only a year later. [2]

Rowley's '*When you see me, you know me*' was no doubt produced about the same time and was first published in 1605 (QA) by Nathaniel Butter. There can be little doubt that it was this piece to which the wellknown entry of an Enterlude on K. Henry VIII., made for Butter on the Stationers' Books in 1604, refers. The buffoonery of the scenes in which King Henry walks the City in disguise, makes the acquaintance of Black Will, and together with him is 'clapped' in the Counter;

---

[1] Only two of these six plays are mentioned by Mr. Allibone, viz. Joshua and Hymen's Holiday.

[2] On this and some other points compare *Jahrbuch der Deutschen Shakespeare-Gesellschaft* IX, 55 seqq.

the prominent part which the two fools take not only in the dialogue, but even in the action of the play (which latter in Shakespeare's plays is nowhere the case); the breeching of Edward Browne, Prince Edward's 'souffre-douleur', may well justify the title of Enterlude given by a careless publisher, although the author on better thought ultimately chose that of a Chronicle-History. The comic parts intrude into the presence-chamber of the King himself, and the King, the Queen and their guest, the Emperor of Germany, are made to crack rather low jokes with the fool, while Shakespeare in his Henry VIII. has raised the whole into a higher sphere of dignity and refinement and has admitted the comic element only where he introduces the crowd, gathered in the streets and in the palace-yard. Perhaps it was just this savouring of the old Enterlude which won such a lasting popularity for Rowley's play, for it was republished in 1613 (QB), 1621 (QC), and 1632 (QD). The Bodleian Library is in possession of all these quartos, whereas the British Museum can only boast of copies of QB and QD. Watt (Bibl. Brit.) only knows QB and QD and Mr. Halliwell (Dict. Old English Plays) only QA and QD; the latter might have known better, if he had compared Lowndes. The three quartos QB, QC, and QD contain 42 leaves each and have 38 lines on each page; in all quartos, with the exception of QA, each page beginning and ending with the same words. Another copy is preserved in the Dyce-Bequest at the South Kensington Museum, but unfortunately the imprint has been cut off, so that only a minute comparison with the Oxford copies can show which edition it is.

The exact titles of the four quartos are as follows:

QA. When you see me You know me Or the famous Chronicle Historie of King Henry the eight, with the birth and vertuous life of Edward Prince of Wales. As it was playd by the high and mightie Prince of Wales his servants. By Samuell Rowly, servant to the Prince. London Imprinted for Nathaniell Butter, and are to be sold in Paules Churchyeard neare Saint Austines gate, 1605. (Bodleian Library, Malone Add. 829.)

QB. The title coincides with that of QA as far as 'servant to the Prince'; it then proceeds: At London, Printed for Nathaniell Butter, and are to be sold at his shop in Paules Church-yard neare S. Austines gate 1613. (Bodleian Library, Malone 186. British Museum C. 34. e. 2.)

QC. A few slight orthographical variations excepted the title is the same as that of QB. 1621. (Bodleian Library, Malone Add. 830).

QD. The title differs only in the imprint, which runs thus: At London, Printed by B.A. and T.F. for Nath: Butter, and are to be sold at his shop in St. Pauls Church-yard, neare St. Austins Gate. 1632. (Bodleian Library, Douce Collection R. 130 [?]. British Museum C. 34. e. 3.)

In the same year with the first quarto Nathaniel Butter brought out Thomas Heywood's *If you know not me, you know nobody*. Not only does this title curiously correspond with that of Rowley's piece, but both are embellished by whole-length woodcuts the one of Henry VIII. (after the wellknown picture by Holbein), the other of Elizabeth The first part of Heywood's play was reprinted simultaneously with that of Rowley in 1613 and 1632 (as also in 1606 and 1608); 'the second part, says Mr. Collier, was originally published in 1606, and reprinted in 1609, 1623, and 1633, all the editions being in 4to. One would think that the title of *If you know not me, you know nobody* was meant to insinuate, that Queen Elizabeth was represented so life-like in the play, that every spectator or reader should know her at once, if he knew any person at all. A different explanation, however, is intimated in the play itself, where Old Hobson, a rich City-merchant, being asked by the Queen: Friend, what are you?, bluntly replies:

Knowest thou not me, Queen? then thou knowest nobody.

Bones a me, Queen, I am Hobson; old Hobson,
By the stocks: I am sure, you know me.¹

It is evident, that Shakespeare's art and genius cannot be fully appreciated, if not compared to the works of his contemporaries, especially when, as it is the case in the present instance, the same subject has been treated. This reason would of itself go far to justify the publication of even subordinate dramatic productions of the Elizabethan age; it is, however, greatly strengthened, if it can be shown or made probable, that a play has stood in some nearer relation to Shakespeare, either as a source, a forerunner, or an imitation. Such a relation seems to have subsisted between Rowley's *When you see me, you know me* and Shakespeare's K. Henry VIII. and will ensure to the former a permanent literary value. It is from this point of view that Mr. Collier in his edition of Armin's Nest of Ninnies (published for the Shakespeare Society) speaks in favour of Rowley's play, 'which, he says, is a singular picture of manners and of the mode, in which, just after the death of Elizabeth, her father was exhibited at the public theatres. In this view *When you see me, you know me* may be said to have a direct relation to the Henry VIII. of our great dramatist and may well deserve to be hereafter reprinted by the Shakespeare Society.' This intention, however, was never realized, but has remained a *pium desiderium*.

Notwithstanding the different spirit that pervades the two works of Shakespeare and Rowley, there are so many striking coincidences between them as to induce us to the belief not only that Shakespeare was acquainted with Rowley's play before it was printed — which may be taken for granted without any argument — but that Rowley's play was acted before Shakespeare wrote his K. Henry VIII. and that Shakespeare took a series of traits from it — traits, which, to tell the truth, with Rowley are nothing but dross, but were turned into gold by the magic hand of Shakespeare.

¹ Mr. Collier's edition, printed for the Shakespeare Society, p. 136.

King Henry, who of course must be first introduced to the reader's notice, with both poets makes frequent use of his favourite ejaculation Ha!, while his favourite oaths 'Mother o' God, Body o' me', &c., no less frequently introduced by Rowley, were suppressed by Shakespeare; by both poets he is exhibited leaning on the shoulder of some one of his intimate courtiers, by both walking in the gallery as was his 'custom always of the afternoon'.[1] Both poets show the king's angry impatience when interrupted in his privacy; the only difference is, that with Rowley it is Wolsey who provokes the king's rage by his impertinence, whereas with Shakespeare (II, 2) the dukes of Suffolk and Norfolk have to 'endure the storm' on such an occasion. The unceremonious intrusion of an overhasty messenger into the king's presence and his angry repulsion by the latter have been transferred by Shakespeare to the dying-scene of Queen Katherine. With Rowley, who is as unceremonious as the messenger himself, the poor fellow is mercilessly kicked out by the king. The incident of the king's sending his ring to Cranmer is also common to both poets. Rowley makes the king say:

> Sir William Compton, here take my ring,
> Bid Doctor Cranmer haste to court again,
> Give him that token of king Henry's love,
> Discharge our guards, we fear no traitor's hand,
> Our state, beloved of all, doth firmly stand;
> Go, Compton.

With Shakespeare the king gives the ring in person with the words (V, 1):

> If entreaties
> Will render you no remedy, this ring
> Deliver them, and your appeal to us
> There make before them.

---

[1] 'Walking in the gallery' seems to have been among the pastimes of Shakespeare's contemporaries; compare The Puritan II, 1: *Mary*: Sir John Pennydub? where? where? *Frailty* He's walking in the gallery.

On the whole the perusal of Rowley's play will satisfy the reader that Shakespeare has bestowed evident care on showing the character of the king in a favourable light. If Queen Elizabeth should have been acquainted with the two dramas 'When you see me, you know me' and King Henry VIII. she must have been shocked by Rowley's portrait of her father, but could not have helped being pleased with his likeness as drawn by 'gentle' Shakespeare.

In the delineation of Cardinal Wolsey no fewer features are common to both poets. With Rowley the fool reproaches the cardinal with keeping 'a fair leman at Charlton', and Shakespeare, who banished the fool from his play, has put the same reproach into the Earl of Surrey's mouth (III, 2):

> I'll startle you
> Worse than the sacring bell, when the brown wench
> Lay kissing in your arms, lord cardinal.

The fatal influence which the cardinal exercises over the king is by both poets ascribed to his wonderful eloquence. With Rowley Wolsey boasts of having 'so won Great England's lord with words'

> That under colour of advising him,
> I overrule both council, court, and king.

In Shakespeare's K. Henry VIII., III, 2 the Lord Chamberlain says:

> If you cannot
> Bar his access to the king, never attempt
> Any thing on him; for he hath a witch-craft
> Over the king in's tongue.

Further on both poets derive the cardinal's downfall almost in the self-same words from the same causes: from his extorting large sums from the people and heaping up immense treasures, with which to attain the last object of his ambition, the papal throne; from the arrogant formula '*Ego et Rex meus*', which Wolsey did not scruple to employ in his correspondence with the pope and foreign princes; and lastly from his impudence in stamping his cardinal's hat on the king's coin. The king in Rowley's play says:

> How durst ye, sirrah, in your embassage,
> Unknown to us, stamp in our royal coin
> The base impression of your cardinal's hat,
> As if you were co-partner of the crown?
> *Ego et Rex meus:* you and your king must be
> In equal state, and pomp, and majesty.

Shakespeare has not only ennobled this rude speech, but has again put forward the Dukes of Norfolk and Suffolk as the mouth-pieces of the king's anger (III, 2):

> *Nor.* Then, that in all you writ to Rome, or else
> To foreign princes: 'Ego et Rex meus'
> Was still inscribed; in which you brought the king
> To be your servant. —
> *Suf.* That, out of mere ambition, you have caused
> Your holy hat to be stamp'd on the king's coin.

Some critics may be inclined to explain these coincidences by the circumstance that both poets borrowed most of their materials from Holinshed, who indeed enumerates the above facts among the charges raised against the cardinal. 'Item, he says, in all writings, which he wrote to Rome, or any other forren prince, he wrote *Ego et Rex meus,* I and my king: as who would saie, that the king were his servant. — — Item, that he caused the cardinal's hat to be put on the kings coin.' This was certainly the common source of both poets, but why did they select from among the long list of charges the very same items for introduction into their plays? And what common source can be found out for those scenes, where the births of the Prince of Wales and Princess Elizabeth are looked forward to and announced? Rowley makes the king say:

> Ladies, attend her! (viz. the queen); Countess of Salisbury! Sister Mary!
> Who first brings word that Henry hath a son
> Shall be rewarded well.

To which the fool adds: 'Ay, I'll be his surety: but do you hear, wenches, she that brings the first tidings, howsoever it fall out, let her be sure to say the child's like his father, or else she shall have nothing'. In strict accordance with this artful precept the old lady in Shakespeare, who bears the message of the queen's delivery, proclaims the likeness in the strongest terms:

'Tis like you
As cherry is to cherry —

whilst Rowley's Countess of Salisbury against the fool's not at all foolish advice contents herself with inviting the king to look at his own flesh and bone and warranting the child his own. Shakespeare's old lady is even mindful of the king's burning desire for a son and therefore first introduces Elizabeth as a boy. The amount of the recompense is not mentioned by Rowley; the king merely says:

Take that for thy good news; &c.

Shakespeare's old lady receives a hundred marks and complains of the insufficiency of this gift in the following violent words:

An hundred marks! By this light, I'll ha' more.
An ordinary groom is for such payment.
I will have more, or scold it out of him.
Said I for this, the girl was like to him?
I will have more, or else unsay't.

Passages of a different, but no less curious character in Rowley are the king's treatment of the page who is putting the garter round his leg and the eulogy on music pronounced by Doctor Tye, the prince of Wales's music-master, inasmuch as these passages find their Shakesperean parallels not in K. Henry VIII., but in the Taming of the Shrew and the Merchant of Venice; the former recalls the wellknown scene where Petruchio is being undressed, the latter the celebrated garden-scene at Belmont. Those, says Doctor Tye, who term music idle, vain, and frivolous, do indeed upbraid it,

and those that do are such
As in themselves no happy concords hold.

All music jars with them; &c.
Shakespeare's wellknown words are these:
>   The man that hath no music in himself,
>   Nor is not moved with concord of sweet sounds,
>   Is fit for treasons, stratagems, and spoils.

Even the legend of Orpheus is touched on by both poets. Rowley says:
>   And if the poet fail us not, my lord,
>   The dulcet tongue of music made the stones
>   To move, irrational beasts and birds to dance &c.

Shakespeare, after expatiating more fully on the influence of music on animals, continues:
>   Therefore the poet
>   Did feign that Orpheus drew trees, stones, and floods.

A marked difference, however, between these two eulogies lies in the stress which Rowley lays on the religious, not to say Christian character of music — he mentions the continual hymns of the Seraphim, the quire of the Angels at the birth of Christ and the dreadful note of the last trumpet — whereas Shakespeare leaves religious music entirely out of the question, a circumstance which ought to be well considered in an examination of his religious sentiments and principles.

Here then the question of priority may best be raised. The *prima facie* impression on the reader will be, that Shakespeare here as elsewhere made use of crude materials and gave them an immortal shape. No critic, I think, will doubt that Rowley's play was in existence some years before it appeared in print, for such was almost invariably the case with all dramatic productions of the Elizabethan age. But however strongly I feel inclined to the belief, that it was anterior to Shakespeare's K. Henry VIII., even if the latter was originally written in 1602—3, yet I am nowise prepared to maintain that it also preceded his Taming of the Shrew and his Merchant of Venice. We are therefore driven to the dilemma, either that Rowley was the borrower of the respective passages, or that these passages originated with both poets independently from each other. We shall hardly be able to arrive at a nearer approach to the truth, as the chronology of Shakespeare's plays is nothing but a network of conjectures and surmises. Thus much, however, may be safely asserted, that both the prologue and epilogue to K. Henry VIII., which probably are of later origin than the play itself, distinctly hint at Rowley's Chronicle-History. What reader of 'When you see me, you know me' can peruse the following lines of Shakespeare's prologue without being struck by the hit on the poet's predecessor?

> Only they
> That come to hear a merry bawdy play,
> A noise of targets, or to see a fellow
> In a long motley coat guarded with yellow,
> Will be deceived; for, gentle hearers, know,
> To rank our chosen truth with such a show
> As fool and fight is, beside forfeiting
> Our own brains, and the opinion that we bring,
> To make that only true we now intend,
> Will leave us never an understanding friend.

The poet — or whoever wrote the prologue — states that 'fool and fight' have been purposely omitted, both of which are characteristic features of Rowley's play, in which King Henry himself is introduced trying his skill with a sword and buckler-man in the streets of London. As 'a merry bawdy play' Rowley's piece might be denounced on account of the indecent speeches in which Will Summers indulges even when conversing with Queen Jane Seymour and Queen Katherine Parr; they are certainly not a whit more bawdy than numerous passages in Shakespeare himself, but they are more repulsive, because there is 'no sallet in the lines.' Even the repeated assertion, that in Shakespeare's play 'all is true', sounds like an indirect reproof of those comic scenes which are merely due to Rowley's own invention. The epilogue adds another innuendo on Rowley in the words that some spectators come

> to hear the city
> Abused extremely, and to cry 'That's witty';

for those spectators who recollected the City-guard and the Counter in Rowley's play, could not but own, that there was no lack of abuse of the City.

Historical truth in Rowley's Chronicle-History is partly strikingly neglected and partly as studiously observed; in both respects it stands side by side with Shakespeare's K. Henry VIII. Shakespeare makes Queen Katherine die three years earlier than she really did and the trial of Cranmer with him takes place a dozen of years before its time, while Rowley gives an additional length of about fourteen or fifteen years to Cardinal Wolsey's life. On the other hand Rowley has drawn even the subordinate characters of Doctor Tye and Will Summers, the king's fool, with an accuracy and truth, which a superficial reader would scarcely dream of. Will Summers' character corresponds throughout with the description given of him by Robert Armin in his 'Nest of Ninnies' on the testimony, as he says, of several old inhabitants of Greenwich who had personally known this favourite fool of K. Henry VIII.[1] As Armin published his 'Nest of Ninnies' three years after Rowley's *When you see me, you know me*, it may indeed be doubted, if the latter has not been amongst his sources for the fool's portrait, although the following lines show him to have been in possession of a store of other materials:

Will Sommers born in Shropshire, as some say,
Was brought to Greenwich on a holy day,
Presented to the king; which foole disdain'd
To shake him by the hand, or else asham'd:
How ere it was, as ancient people say,
With much adoe was wonne to it that day.
Leane he was, hollow eyde, as all report,
And stoop he did, too; yet in all the court
Few men were more belou'd then was this foole,

---

[1] Fools and Jesters; with a Reprint of Robert Armin's Nest of Ninnies (1608). Edited by J. P. Collier for the Shakespeare-Society (1842) p. 45.

Whose merry prate kept with the king much rule.
When he was sad, the king and he would rime:
Thus Will exiled sadness many a time.
I could describe him as I did the rest,
But in my mind I doe not think it best:
My reason this; how ere I doe descry him,
So many knew him that I may belye him;
Therefore, to please all people, one by one,
I hold it best to let that paines alone:
Onely this much, — hee was a poor mans friend,
And helpt the widdow often in the end.
The king would euer grant what he would craue,
For well he knew Will no exacting knave:
But whisht the king to doe good deeds great store,
Which caus'd the court to loue him more and more.

That Will Summers was a most honest and disinterested man, and therefore respected both by the court and the people is granted on all hands; he never would ask a favour for himself, but, says Armin (p. 46), 'laid him downe among the spaniels to sleep.' According to the same authority he 'never loved' the cardinal, 'indeed he could never abide him', for he knew him to be neither true to the king, nor generous and humane to the poor. In the opinion of Mr. W. J. Thoms, Will Summers 'owes his reputation rather to the uniform kindness with which he used his influence over bluff Harry, than to his wit or folly. Indeed it may be owing to this circumstance, that, notwithstanding Henry's well-known fondness for these motley followers, Will is almost the only one of them whose memory has survived.'[1]

'A collection was made, says Mr. Collier,[2] of Will Summer's jests, but when it was first printed, is not ascertained. A copy in 1676, has for title, "A pleasant History of the Life and Death of Will Summers; how he came first to be known

---

[1] Fools and Jesters &c. p. 64.
[2] A Select Collection of Old Plays (1825) IX, 14, Note 14.

at court, and by what means he got to be King Henry the Eighth's Jester." It was reprinted by Harding, in 1794, with an engraving from an old portrait, supposed to be Will Summer; but if it be authentic, it does not at all support Armin's description of him, that he was „lean and hollow-eyed" Many of the jests are copied from the French and Italian; and some of them have been assigned also to Scoggin and Tarlton. One or two of these are introduced into S. Rowley's *"When you see me, you know me".*'

'Armin's description of Sommers's person, according to the above cited note by Mr. Thoms, accords very well with the rare print of him by Delaram, described by Granger in his "Biographical History of England" (I. p. 116, ed. 1779), and also with the portrait of him in the frontispiece to the first volume of Sir Henry Ellis's "Original Letters illustrative of English History", which is taken from Henry the Eight's Psalter, preserved among the Royal Mss. in the British Museum. It does not, however, by any means correspond with the admirable picture by Holbein of a merry knave looking through a leaded casement, described in the Guide to the Pictures at Hampton Court, as one of Henry the Eight's jesters, but traditionally said to be a portrait of Will Sommers.'

Rowley was not the first to bring Will Summers on the stage; already in Nash's *'Summer's Last Will and Testament'* (acted in 1592) he plays a prominent part as a looker-on and critic of the dramatic performance after the fashion of Christopher Sly in the Taming of the Shrew, but his remarks lack genial humour and comic vigour. As it appears, Nash's 'show' was performed by the Children of the Chapel and the actor of Summers' part, whose name was Toy, was the only grown-up person amongst them; the epilogue was spoken by a child sitting on his knees and carried off the stage after its delivery.[1]

---

[1] See Mr. Collier's note, Select Collection of Old Plays, IX, 50 seq.

Rowley's Chronicle-History is remarkable as being perhaps the only play in which two domestic fools are introduced, for besides Will Summers we also make the acquaintance of the cardinal's fool, Patch. This appellative noun seems sometimes to have served as a *nomen proprium* for the designation of individual fools, as these poor fellows may frequently have been glad to drop their family names and the households of their masters did not care to know them. According to Douce (Illustrations, 1839, p. 158 seq.) cardinal Wolsey had two fools, both of them named Patch, one of whom he presented to the king.[1] The real name of this fool is said to have been Williams, while that of the other was Sexton. This is shown by the following epigram of John Heywood (First Hundred, Epigr. 44) entitled 'A saying of Patch my lord Cardinal's Foole'.

Maister Sexton, a person of unknowen witte,
As he at my lord Cardinal's boord did sitte,
Greedily raught at a goblet of wine:
Drink none, sayd my lord, for that sore leg of thyne:
I warrant your Grace, quoth Sexton, I provide
For my leg: for I drink on the tother side.[2]

The following text has been constituted from QB and QD; the latter contains a number of welcome corrections — although most of them could scarcely have been missed by any editor — but at the same time adds some fresh misprints and blunders to those by which QB is defaced. In many cases the metre has been spoiled and mangled, sometimes beyond the hope of recovery, while the prose-scenes are printed with an almost unexceptionable correctness. The charge cannot be laid at the author's door, as no poet, however subordinate, can be believed to have written such limping verses. I have therefore now and then been driven to propose remedies which I am afraid conservative critics will think rather bold; yet I have carefully refrained from altering the peculiarities of the poet's language, such as the construction of the noun

[1] See Cavendish, Life of Cardinal Wolsey ed. by Singer I, 191 and 343.
[2] Warton, H. E. P. (1840) III, 87. See also Nares s. Patch.

in the plural form with what is now considered the singular of the verb, to which construction the author seems addicted as to an almost binding rule. The remark which Mr. Abbot has made on this point ought not to pass unheeded. 'The third person plural in —s, he says[1], is extremely common in the Folio. It is generally altered by modern editors, so that its commonness has not been duly recognized. Fortunately, there are some passages where the rhyme or metre has made alteration impossible.' Another metrical peculiarity of Rowley is the regular dissolution of the final — *ion* in the end of the line, which, as I have had occasion to remark elsewhere, occurs with little less regularity in Chapman's Tragedy of Alphonsus.[2] There are hardly three or four exceptions in Rowley and I doubt very much, if the respective lines should not be read as verses of six feet, so that there would be no exception at all.

In common with a great number of Elizabethan plays '*When you see me, you know me*' is not divided into acts and scenes, a defect which I have not deemed it advisable to remedy, but have only added a list of the Dramatis Personæ. The stage-directions too are very defective and frequently misplaced.

Before concluding it may be as well to glance at the only other play of Sam. Rowley which has been preserved in print. '*The Noble Souldier*', or, as the heading of the pages has it, '*The Noble Spanish Souldier*' appeared, as we have seen, in 1634 and according to Lowndes was reprinted in 1637. The title of the first edition runs thus: 'The Noble Souldier. Or, A Contract broken, Justly Reveng'd. A Tragedy. Written by S. R. — Non est, Lex Iustior Ulla, Quam Nescis Artifices, Arte perire Sua. London: Printed for Nicholas Vavasour, and are to be sold at his shop in the Temple, neere the Church. 1634.'[3] Since I have alluded before to the Printer's preface

---

[1]Shakespearian Grammar (3d Ed.) 533.

[2]See my edition of that play (Leipzig, 1867) p. 37. Compare also Mr. Abbott's Shakespearian Grammar 479.

[3]The copy in the British Museum bears the pressmark 644. c. 15. — According to Mr. Halliwell (Dict. Old English Plays) Nicholas Vavasour

INTRODUCTION.   xix

to this play as affording some clue to the time when the author may be presumed to have died, and as the book has never been reprinted, the reader will perhaps thank me for transcribing the whole of this preface. It is to the following effect:

'The Printer to the Reader. Understanding Reader, I present this to your view, which has received applause in Action. The Poet might conceive a compleat satisfaction upon the Stages approbation: But the Printer rests not there, knowing that that which was acted and approved upon the Stage might bee no lesse acceptable in Print. It is now communicated to you whose leisure and knowledge admits of reading and reason: Your Judgement now this *Posthumus*[1] assures himselfe will well attest his predecessors endeavours to give content to men of the ablest quality, such as intelligent readers are here conceived to be. I could have troubled you with a longer Epistle, but I feare to stay you from the booke, which affords better words and matter than I can. So the work modestly depending in the skale [sic!] of your Judgement, the Printer for his part craves your pardon, hoping by his promptnesse to doe you greater service, as conveniency shall enable him to give you more or better testimony of his cutirenesse towards you. N. V.'

Perhaps it is also owing to the printer that the play is divided into acts and scenes and furnished with the following list of the Dramatis Personæ.

King of Spaine.
Cardinall.
Duke of Medina
Marquesse Daenia
Alba   } Dons of Spayne.
Roderigo
Valasco
Lopez

entered this play on the Stationers' Registers on the 9th of December 1633, under its running-title, as written by Thomas Decker.

[1] The italics are the printer's.

Queene, a Florentine.
ONAELIA, Neece to MEDINA, the Contracted Lady.
SEBASTIAN, her Sonne.
MALATESTE, a Florentine.
BALTAZAR, the Souldier.
A Poet.
COCKADILLIO, a foolish Courtier.
A Fryer.

The contents of 'The Noble Soldier' are interesting only inasmuch as they throw a striking light on the popular opinion of Shakespeare's time regarding troth-plight and precontract. The king of Spain is represented as having plighted his troth to the noble Onælia, by whom he has a son. He, however, partly by a shameless fraud, partly by force, snatches his written promise of marriage from her and marries a Florentine princess, whom all the characters of the play, the catholic clergy not excepted, denounce as a strumpet, while they persist in considering Onælia the lawful wife of the king and her son his legitimate heir. They will not be satisfied, till, as the Duke of Medina expresses it (sign. E, 2):

> they ha' forc'd him
> To cancell his late lawless bond he seal'd
> At the high Altar to his Florentine Strumpet,
> And in his bed lay this his troth-plight wife.

The foremost champion of Onælia and her claims is Baltazar, the Noble Soldier. The king however is obstinate; he wants to marry Onælia to one of his courtiers and directs her son to be murdered, but is himself poisoned at Onælia's weddingfeast and repents before his death, his last consolation being to learn that his son Sebastian has not been killed, but comes to witness the last moments of his dying father, who amidst the universal approbation of all the court appoints him his successor. The popular notions of the validity and sanctity of troth-plight, which are so forcibly put forward in this tragedy, must above all be borne in mind, when we attempt to form an opinion of Shakespeare's marriage; irregular as it was, it was yet preceded by troth-plight and those commentators who have pleaded this circumstance in the poet's favour might have added Rowley's *Noble Soldier* to the number of their arguments. It is also well known that the precontract into which Anne Boleyn was said to have entered with some person unknown — for Northumberland denied upon oath that he had ever stood in any such relation to the queen — was alleged as an argument against the validity of her marriage with the king. In the same manner in the case of Anne of Cleves a precontract with the Count of Lorraine was alluded to as a lawful impediment to her marriage with Henry VIII., although the documents relating to this precontract could never be procured from Germany.[1] We may perhaps be justified in considering these two memorable and notorious cases, more especially the former, as one of the links, by which in the author's mind the tragedy of '*The Noble Soldier*' was connected with his Chronicle-History of '*When you see me, you know me.*'

---

[1] See Froude (1858) II, 502. III, 464 and 485.

WHEN YOU SEE ME, YOU KNOW ME.

Or the famous Chronicle Historic of King Henrie the Eight,
With the Birth and vertuous Life of Edward Prince of Wales.

As it was playd

By the high and mightie Prince of Wales his servants.

By

SAMVELL ROVVLY,
Servant to the Prince.

DRAMATIS PERSONÆ.

KING HENRY the Eighth.
CHARLES the Fifth, Emperor of Germany.
EDWARD, Prince of Wales.
CHARLES BRANDON, Duke of Suffolk.
LORD SEYMOUR, Father to Queen Jane
LORD DUDLEY.
LORD GRAY.
The young MARQUESS OF DORSET.
SIR WILLIAM COMPTON.
CARDINAL WOLSEY.
CARDINAL CAMPEIUS, Legate from the Pope.
BONNER, afterwards Bishop of London.
GARDINER, afterwards Bishop of Winchester.
DOCTOR CRANMER.
BONNIVET, High Admiral of France } Ambassadors from France.
JOHN DE MAZO, Bishop of Paris }
DOCTOR TYE.
Young EDWARD BROWNE.
ROKESBY, Groom of the Wardrobe
WILL SUMMERS, Fool to the king.
PATCH, Fool to Cardinal Wolsey
A Messenger.
A Constable.
PRICHALL, CAPCASE, DORMOUSE, &c., Watchmen.
BLACK WILL.
Keeper, Porter, and Prisoners in the Counter.

QUEEN JANE SEYMOUR.
QUEEN KATHARINE PARR.
LADY MARY, sister to K. Henry.
COUNTESS OF SALISBURY.

        Ladies, Attendants, and Servants.

Enter the CARDINAL *with the* AMBASSADORS OF FRANCE, *in all state and royalty, the Purse and Mace before him.*

Wol. Gentlemen, give leave! You great ambassadors
From Francis, the most Christian king of France,
My Lord of Paris and Lord Bonnivet,
Welcome to England! Since the king your master
Entreats our furtherance to advance his peace,
Giving us titles of high dignity,
As next elect to Rome's supremacy,
Tell him, we have so wrought with English Henry
(Who as his right hand loves the cardinal)
That undelayed you shall have audience,
And this day will the king in person sit
To hear your message and to answer it.
   Bonniv. Your grace hath done us double courtesy,
For so much doth the king our master long
To have an answer of this ambassage,
As minutes are thought months till we return.
   Paris. And that's the cause his highness moves your grace
To quick dispatch betwixt the king and him,
And for a quittance of your forwardness
And hopeful kindness to the crown of France,
Twelve reverend bishops are sent post to Rome,
Both from his highness and the emperor,
To move Campeius and the cardinals
For your election to the papal throne,
That Wolsey's head may wear the triple crown.
   Wol. We thank his highness for rememb'ring us,
And so salute my lord the emperor,
Both which (if Wolsey be made Pope of Rome)
Shall be made famous through all christendom.
                      Enter BONNER.
How now, Bonner?

  Bon. Sir William Compton from his highness comes
To do a message to your excellence.
  Wol. Delay him awhile and tell him we are busy.
Meantime, my lords, you shall withdraw yourselves;
Our private conference must not be known.
Let all your gentlemen in their best array
Attend you bravely to king Henry's court,
Where we in person presently will meet you,
And doubt not we'll prevail successfully.
  Bonniv. But hath your grace yet mov'd his highness' sister
For kind acceptance of our sovereign's love?
  Wol. I have, and by the king's means finish'd it,
And yet it was a task, I tell ye, lords,
That might have been impos'd to Hercules,
To win a lady of her spirit and years
To see her first love crown'd with silver hairs,
As old king Lewis is, that bedrid lies,
Unfit for love or worldly vanities.
  Bonniv. But 't is his country's peace the king respects.
  Wol. We think no less and we have fully wrought it.
The emperor's forces that were levied
To invade the frontiers of Low Burgundy,
Are stayed in Brabant by the king's command.
The Admiral Hayward that was lately sent,
With threescore sail of ships and pinnaces,
To batter down the towns in Normandy,
Is by our care for him call'd home again:
Then doubt not of a fair successful end,
Since Wolsey is esteem'd your sovereign's friend.
  Paris. We thank your excellence and take our leaves.
  Wol. Haste ye to court, I'll meet ye presently.
  Bonniv. Good morrow to your grace.   [*Exeunt.*
  Wol. Good morrow, lords. Go, call Sir William Compton in.
We must have narrow eyes and quick conceit
To look into these dangerous stratagems;
I will effect for France, as they for me.
If Wolsey to the pope's high state attain,
The league is kept, or else he'll break 't again.
     Enter BONNER *and* COMPTON.
Now, good Sir William?
  Comp. The king, my lord, entreats your reverend grace,
There may be had some private conference
Betwixt his highness and your excellence,

Before he hear the French ambassadors,
And wills you hasten your repair to him.
    Wol. We will attend his highness presently.
Bonner, see all our train be set in readiness,
That in our state and pomp pontifical
We may pass on to grace King Henry's court.
    Comp. I have a message from the queen, my lord,
Who much commends and humbly thanks your grace
For your exceeding love and zealous prayers,
By your directions through all England sent,
To invocate for her sound prosperous help,
By heaven's fair hand, in child-bed passions.
    Wol. We thank her highness, that accepts our love;
In all cathedral churches through the land
Are masses, dirges, and professions sung,
With prayers to heaven to bless her majesty
And send her joy, and quick delivery.
And so, Sir William, do my duty to her:
Queen Jane was ever kind and courteous
And always of her subjects honoured.
    Comp. I take my leave, my lord.   [*Exit.*
    Wol. Adieu, good knight, we'll follow presently.
Now, Wolsey, work thy wits like gads of steel,
And make them pliable to all impressions,
That king and queen and all may honour thee.
So toil'd not Cæsar in the state of Rome,
As Wolsey labours in th' affairs of kings;
As Hannibal with oil did melt the Alps,
To make a passage into Italy,
So must we bear our high-pitch'd eminence,
To dig for glory in the hearts of men,
Till we have got the papal diadem.
And to this end have I compos'd this plot,
And made a league between the French and us,
And match'd their aged king in holy marriage
With Lady Mary, royal Henry's sister,
That he, in peace complotting with the emperor,
May plead for us within the courts of Rome.
Wherefore was Alexander's fame so great,
But that he conquer'd and deposed kings?
And where doth Wolsey fail to follow him,
That thus commandeth kings and emperors?
Great England's lord have I so won with words,

That, under colour of advising him,
I overrule both council, court, and king.
Let him command, but we will execute,
Making our glory to out-shine his fame,
Till we have purchas'd an eternal name.

Enter BONNER.

Now, Bonner, are those proclamations sent,
As we directed, to the shrieves of London
Of certain new devised articles
For ordering those brothels call'd the Stewes?
    Bon. They are ready, my lord, and the shrieve attends
                                          for them.
    Wol. Dispatch him quickly and haste after me,
We must attend the king's high majesty.

Sound trumpets. Enter KING HENRY *the Eighth;* QUEEN JANE *big with child; the* CARDINAL; CHARLES BRANDON, DUKE OF SUFFOLK; DUDLEY; GRAY; COMPTON; *the* LADY MARY; *the* COUNTESS OF SALISBURY, *attending on the Queen.*

    King. Charles Brandon, Dudley, and my good Lord Gray,
Prepare yourselves and be in readiness
To entertain these French ambassadors;
Meet them before our royal palace gate,
And so conduct them to our majesty;
We mean this day to give them audience.
    Dud. Gray. We will, my lord.
    Bran.   Let one attend without,
And bring us word when they are coming on.
    King. How now, Queen Jane? Mother of God, my love,
Thou wilt never be able to sit half this time.
Ladies, I fear she'll wake you ere't be long,
Methinks she bears her burden very heavily,
And yet, good sister, and my honour'd lords,
If this fair hour exceed not her expect,
And pass the calendar of her accounts,
She'll hear this embassage — Jane, wilt thou not?
    Qu. Jane. Yes, my dear lord; I cannot leave your sight,
So long as life retains this mansion,
In whose sweet looks bright sovereignty's enthroned,
That make all nations love and honour thee;
Within thy frame sits awful majesty,
Wreath'd in the curled furrows of thy front:

Admir'd and fear'd even of thine enemies.
To be with thee is my felicity;
Not to behold the state of all the world,
Could win thy queen, thy sick, unwieldy queen,
To leave her chamber in this mother's state,
But sight of thee, unequall'd potentate.

   King. God-a-mercy, Jane, reach me thy princely hand:
Thou art now a right woman, goodly, chief of thy sex,
Methinks thou art a queen superlative.
Mother o' God, this is a woman's glory,
Like good September vines, loaden with fruit.
How ill did they define the name of woman,
Adding so foul a preposition,
To call it woe to man, 'tis woe from man,
If woe it be; and, then, who does not know,
That women still from men receive their woe?
Yet they love men for it, but what's their gain?
Poor fools! no more but travail for their pain.
Come, love, thou art sad: call Will Summers in,
To make her merry; where's the fool to-day?

   Dud. He was met, my liege, they say at London
Early this morning with doctor Skelton.

   King. He's ne'er from thence; go, let a groom be sent
And fetch him home. My good lord cardinal,
Who are the chief of these ambassadors?

   Wol. Lord Bonnivet, the French High Admiral,
And John de Mazo, reverend Bishop of Paris.

   King. Let their welcome be thy care good Wolsey.

   Wol. It shall, my liege.

Enter COMPTON.

   King. Spare for no cost. Compton, what news?

   Comp. Th' ambassadors, my liege.

   King. Enough; go, give them entertainment. Lord!
Charles Brandon, hear'st thou? Give them courtesy
Enough, and state enough; go and conduct them.

   Bran. I go, my lord.

   Enter WILL SUMMERS *booted and spurred, blowing a horn.*

   King. How now, William? What, post post? Where have you been riding?

   Will. Out of my way, old Harry. Im am all on the spur, I can tell ye, I have tidings worth telling.

King. Why, where hast thou been?

Will. Marry, I rise early and ride post to London, to know what news was here at court.

King. Was that your nearest way, William?

Will. O, ay, the very foot-path; but yet I rid the horse-way to hear it. I warrant there is ne'er a conduit-head keeper in London, but knows what is done in all the courts of christendom.

Wol. And what is the best news there, William?

Will. Good news for you, my lord cardinal, for one of the old women waterbearers told me for certain, that last Friday all the bells in Rome rang backward: there was a thousand dirges sung, six hundred Avemaries said, every man washed his face in holy water, the people crossing and blessing themselves to send them a new pope, for the old is gone to Purgatory.

Wol. Ha, ha, ha.

Will. Nay, my lord, you'ld laugh, if it were so, indeed, for every body thinks, if the pope were dead, you gape for a benefice; but this news, my lord, is called too good to be true.

King. But this news came apace, Will, that came from Rome to London since Friday last.

Will. For 'twas at Billingsgate by Saturday morning, 'twas a full moon, and it came up in a spring tide.

King. Then you heard of the ambassadors that are come.

Will. Ay, ay, and that was the cause of my riding, to know what they came for; I was told it all at a barber's.

King. Ha, ha! what a fool's this, Jane; and what do they say he comes for, Will?

Will. Marry, they say he comes to crave thy aid against the great Turk that vows to over-run all France within this fortnight, he's in a terrible rage belike, and they say the reason is, his old god Mahomet that was buried i'th' top on's church at Mecca, his tomb fell down and kill'd a sow and seven pigs, whereupon they think all swines flesh is new sanctified, and now it is thought the Jews will fall to eating of pork extremely after it.

King. This is strange indeed, but is this all?

Will. No, there is other news that was told me among the women at a bake-house, and that is this: they say, the great bell in Glastonbury has tolled twice, and that king Arthur and his knights of the round table that were buried in armour, are alive again, crying Saint George for England, and mean shortly to conquer Rome. Marry, this is thought to be but a moral.

King. The ambassadors are coming; and hear, William, see that you be silent, when you see them here.

Will. I'll be wise and say little, I warrant thee, and therefore, till I see them come, I'll go talk with the queen. How dost thou, Jane? Sirrah Harry, she looks very big upon me, but I care not, an she bring thee a young prince: Will Summers may haps be his fool, when you two are both dead and rotten.

King. Go to, William. How now, Jane? what, groaning? God's me, thou hast an angry soldier's frown.

Will. I think so, Harry: thou hast pressed her often. I am sure this two years she has served under thy standard.

Qu. Jane. Good faith, my lord, I must entreat your grace,
That, with your favour, I may leave the presence;
I cannot stay to hear this embassage.

King. God's holy mother! Ladies, lead her to her chamber;
Go bid the midwives and the nurses wait,
Make wholesome fires and take her from the air.
Now, Jane, God! bring me but a chopping boy,
Be but a mother to a prince of Wales
And a ninth Henry to the English crown,
And thou mak'st full my hopes. Fair queen, adieu,
And may heaven's helping hand our joys renew.

Comp. God make your majesty a happy mother!

Dud. And help you in your weakest passions!
With zealous prayer we all will invocate
The powers divine for your delivery.

Qu. Jane. We thank ye all, and in fair interchange
We'll pray for you. Now, on my humble knees,
I take my leave of your high majesty:
God send your highness long and happy reign,
And bless this kingdom and your subjects' lives,
And to your gracious heart all joy restore!
I fear I never shall behold you more.

King. Do not think so, fair queen; go to thy bed.
Let not my love be so discomforted.

Will. No, no, I warrant thee, Jane, make haste and dispatch this, that thou may'st have another against next Christmas.

King. Ladies, attend her! Countess of Salisbury! sister Mary!

Who first brings word that Harry hath a son,
Shall be rewarded well.

Will. Ay, I'll be his surety: but do you hear, wenches, she that brings the first tidings, howsoever it fall out, let her be sure to say the child's like his father, or else she shall have nothing.

Enter LORDS *and* AMBASSADORS.

King. Welcome, Lord Bonnivet! welcome, bishop!
What from our brother brings this embassage?

Bonniv. Most fair commends, great and renowned Henry.
We, in the person of our lord and king,
Here of your highness do entreat a league,
And to re-edify the former peace,
Held 'twixt the realms of England and of France,
Of late disordered, for some petty wrongs;
And pray your majesty to stay your powers,
Already levied in Low Burgundy;
Which to maintain our oaths shall be engaged,
And to confirm it with more surety,
He craves your fair consent unto his love,
And give the Lady Mary for his queen,
The second sister to your royal self.
So may an heir, springing from both your bloods,
Make both realms happy by a lasting league.

King. We kindly do receive your master's love;
And yet our grant stands strong unto his suit,
If that no following censure feeble it:
For we herein must take our council's aid.
But howsoever, our answer shall be swift.
Meantime we grant you fair access to woo
And win her (if you can) to be his queen;
Ourself will second you. Right welcome both!
Lord cardinal, these lords shall be your guests,
But let our treasure waste to welcome them:
Banquet them, how they will, what cheer, what sport,
Let them see, Harry keeps a kingly court.

Wol. I shall, my sovereign.

King. Withdraw awhile, ourselves we'll follow ye.

[*Exeunt Wolsey and Ambassadors.*

Now, Will, are you not deceiv'd in this embassage?
You heard, they came for aid against the Turk.

Will. Well then, now I see, there is loud lies told in London; but all's one, for their coming is to as much purpose as the other.

King. And why, I pray?

Will. Why, dost thou think thy sister such a fool to marry such an old *Dies Veneris* to get her with prince? Ay, when either I, or the cardinal, prove pope, and that will never be, I hope.

King. How knowest thou him to be old, thou never sawest him?

Will. No, nor he me, but I saw his picture with ne'er a tooth i' th' head on't, and all his beard as well favoured as a white frost; but it is no matter, if he have her: he will die shortly, and then she may help to bury him.

Enter Ladies.

First Lady. Run, run, good madam, call the ladies in: call for more woman's help, the queen is sick.

Sec. Lady. For God's love, go back again, and warm more clothes, and let the wine be well burned, I charge ye.

Will. Ay, in any case, or I cannot drink it. Dost thou hear, Harry, what a coil they keep? I warrant, these women will drink thee up more wine with their gossiping than was spent in all the conduits at thy coronation.

Enter LADY MARY *and the* COUNTESS OF SALISBURY.

King. 'Tis no matter, Will. How now, ladies?

L. Mary. I beseech your grace, command the fool forth of the presence.

King. Away, William! you must be gone, here's woman's matters in hand.

Will. Let them speak low then. I'll not out of the room, sure.

Count. Sal. Come, come, let's thrust him out, he'll not stir else.

Will. Thrust me? Nay, an ye go on thrusting, I'll thrust some of you down, I warrant ye.

King. Nay, go, good William.

Will. I'll out of their company, Harry; they will scratch worse than cats, if they catch me, therefore I'll hence and leave. Good bye, ladies!

Do you hear, Madam Mary?
You had need to be wary,
My news is worth a white cake:
You must play at tennis

With old Saint Denis,
And your maidenhead must lie at the stake. [*Exit.*

King. Ha, ha! The fool tells you true, my gentle sister.
But to our business: how fares my queen?
How fares my Jane? has she a son for me,
To raise again our kingdom's sovereignty?

L. Mary. That yet rests doubtful, O my princely lord!
Your poor distressed queen lies weak and sick,
And be it son or daughter, dear she buys it,
Even with her dearest life, for one must die.
All woman's help is past. Then, good my liege,
Resolve it quickly, if the queen shall live.
The child must die, or if it life receive,
You must your hapless queen of life bereave.

King. You pierce me with your news. Run, send for help,
Spend the revenues of my crown for aid,
To save the life of my beloved queen.
How happed, she is so ill attended on,
That we are put to this extremity,
To save the mother, or the child to die?

Count. Sal. I beseech your grace, resolve immediately.

King. Immediately, sayst thou? O, 'tis no quick resolve
Can give good verdict in so sad a choice:
To lose my queen, that is my sum of bliss,
More virtuous than a thousand kingdoms be;
And should I lose my son (if son it be)
That all my subjects so desire to see,
I lose the hope of this great monarchy.
What shall I do?

L. Mary. Remember the queen, my lord.

King. I not forget her, sister. O poor soul!
But I forget thy pain and misery.
Go, let the child die, let the mother live,
Heaven's powerful hand may more children give.
Away and comfort her with our reply,
Harry will have his queen, though thousands die.
[*Exeunt ladies.*

I know no issue of her princely womb:
Why then should I prefer't before her life,
Whose death ends all my hopeful joys on earth?
God's will be done, for sure it is his will,
For secret reasons to himself best known.
Perhaps he did mould forth a son for me

And seeing (that sees all in his creation)
To be some impotent and coward spirit,
Unlike the figure of his royal father,
Has thus decreed, least he should blur our fame,
As whilome did the sixth king of my name
Lose all his father (the fifth Henry) won;
I'll thank the heavens for taking such a son.
Who's within there?

Enter COMPTON.

 Comp. My lord?
 King. Go, Compton, bid Lord Seymour come to me,
The honoured father of my woful queen. [*Exit Compton.*

Enter LADY MARY *with Attendants.*

How now, what news?
 L. Mary. We did deliver what your highness will'd,
Which was no sooner by her grace receiv'd,
But with the sad report she seemed as dead,
Which caused us stay; after recovery
She sent us back to entreat your majesty,
As ever you did take delight in her,
As you prefer the quiet of her soul,
That now is ready to forsake this life,
As you desire to have the life of one:
She doth entreat your grace that she may die,
Least both do perish in this agony:
For to behold the infant suffer death
Were endless tortures, made to stop her breath.
'Then to my lord, quoth she, thus gently say:
The child is fair, the mother earth and clay.'
 King. Sad messenger of woe! O my poor queen,
Canst thou so soon consent to leave this life,
So precious to our soul, so dear to all,
To yield the hopeful issue of thy loins,
To raise our second comfort? Well, be it so!
Ill, be it so! Stay, I revoke my word,
But that, you say, helps not, for she must die:
Yet, if ye can save both, I'll give my crown,
Nay, all I have, and enter bonds for more,
Which with my conquering sword, with fury bent,
I'll purchase in the farthest continent.
Use all your chiefest skill! Make haste, away!
Whilst we for your success devoutly pray. [*Exeunt ladies.*

Enter LORD SEYMOUR.

Sey. All joy and happiness betide my sovereign!
King. Joy be it, good Lord Seymour, noble father!
Or joy, or grief, thou hast a part in it.
Thou com'st to greet us in a doubtful hour,
Thy daughter and my queen lies now in pain,
And if I lose, Seymour, thou canst not gain.
Sey. Get comfort, good my liege, 'tis woman's woe;
Why, 'tis as certain to her as her death,
Both given her in her first creation:
It is a sour to sweet, given them at first
By their first mother; then put sorrow hence,
Your grace ere long shall see a gallant prince.
King. Be thou a prophet, Seymour! In thy words
Thy love some comfort to our hopes affords.

Enter COUNTESS OF SALISBURY *with another lady.*

How now?
Count. Sal. My gracious lord, here I present to you
A goodly son: see here your flesh and bone!
Look, royal lord, I warrant 'tis your own.
Sey. See here, my liege, by the rood, a gallant prince!
King. Ha! little cakebread! 'Fore God, a chopping boy!
Even now I wept with sorrow, now with joy.
Take that for thy good news. How fares my queen?

Enter LADY MARY *with another lady.*

Count. Sal. O my good lord, the woful —
King. Tell me no more of woe! Speak, doth she live?
What weep ye all? Nay, then my heart misgives:
Resolve me, sister! Is the news worth hearing?
L. Mary. Not worth the telling, royal sovereign.
King. Now, by my crown, thou dimst my royalty,
And with thy cloudy looks eclips'st my joys.
Thy silent eye bewrays a ruthful sound
Stopp'd in the organs of thy troubled spirit:
Say, is she dead?
L. Mary. Without offence, she is.
King. Without offence, sayst thou? Heaven take my soul,
What can be more offensive to my life,
Than sad remembrance of my fair queen's death?
Thou woful man that cam'st to comfort me,
How shall I ease thy heart's calamity,
That cannot help myself? How one sad minute

Hath raised a fount of sorrows in his eyes
And bleared his aged cheeks! Yet, Seymour, see,
She's left part of herself, a son to me,
To thee a grandchild, to the land a prince,
The perfect substance of his royal mother,
In whom her memory shall ever live.
Phœnix Jana obiit, nato Phœnice: dolendum,
Secula phœnices nulla tulisse duas.
One phœnix dying, gives another life:
Thus must we flatter our extremest grief.
What day is this?
  Comp.   Saint Edward's even, my lord.
  King. Prepare for christening: Edward shall be his name!
                    [Exeunt.

  Enter the CARDINAL, AMBASSADORS, BONNER, *and* GARDINER.

  Wol. My lords of France, you 've had small cheer with us,
But you must pardon us, the times are sad,
And sorts not now for mirth and banqueting:
Therefore I pray you, make your swift return,
Commend me to your king and kindly tell him,
The English cardinal will remain his friend.
The Lady Mary shall be forthwith sent
And overtake ye, ere you reach to Dover;
And for the business that concerns the league,
Urge it no more, but leave it to my care.
  Bonner. We thank your grace, my good lord cardinal,
And so with thankfulness we take our leaves.
  Wol. Happily speed, my honourable lords,
My heart, I swear, still keeps you company.
Farewell to both, and pray your king remember
My suit betwixt him and the emperor:
We shall be thankful, if they think on us.
  Par. We will be earnest in your cause, my lord,
So of your grace we once more take our leaves.
  Wol. Again farewell. Bonner, conduct them forth.
                    [Exeunt.
Now, Gardiner, what think'st thou of these times?
  Gar. Well, that the league's confirmed, my gracious lord:
Ill, that I fear the death of good queen Jane
Will cause new trouble in our state again.
  Wol. Why think'st thou so?
  Gar. I fear, false Luther's doctrine's spread so far,

Least that his highness, now unmarried,
Should match amongst that sect of Lutherans.
You saw, how soon his majesty was won
To scorn the pope, and Rome's religion,
When queen Anne Bullen wore the diadem.
    Wol. Gardiner, 'tis true; so was the rumour spread,
But Wolsey wrought such means, she lost her head.
Tush! Fear not thou! Whilst Harry's life doth stand,
He shall be king, but we will rule the land.

              Re-enter BONNER.

Bonner, come hither! You are our trusty friend.
See that the treasure we have gathered,
The copes, the vestments, and the chalices,
The smoke-pence, and the tributary fees,
That English chimneys pay the church of Rome,
Be barrel'd close within the inner cellar;
We'll send it over shortly, to prepare
Our swift advancement to Saint Peter's chair.
Be trusty and be sure of honours speedily:
The king hath promis'd, at the next election,
Bonner shall have the bishopric of London.
    Bon. I humbly thank your grace.
    Wol. And Gardiner shall be Lord of Winchester.
Had we our hopes, what shall you not be then,
When we have got the papal diadem?   [*Exeunt.*

    Enter BRANDON, DUDLEY, GRAY, SEYMOUR, COMPTON.

    Bran. How now, Sir William Compton? Where's the king?
    Comp. His grace is walking in the gallery,
As sad and passionate as e'er he was.
    Dud. 'Twere good, your grace went in to comfort him.
    Bran. Not I, Lord Dudley, by my George, I swear:
Unless his highness first had sent for me,
I will not put my head in such a hazard;
I know his anger and his spleen too well.
    Gray. 'Tis strange, this humour has his highness held
Ever since the death of good queen Jane,
That none dares venture to confer with him.

    Enter CARDINAL, SUMMERS, *and* PATCH.

    Dud. Here comes the cardinal.
    Bran. Ay, and two fools after him, his lordship is well attended still.

Sey. Let's win this prelate to salute the king,
It may perhaps work his disgrace with him.
  Wol. How now, William? What, are you here too?
  Will. Ay, my lord, all the fools follow you. I come to bid my cousin Patch welcome to the court, and when I come to York House, he'll do as much for me: will ye not, Patch?
  Patch. Yes, cousin. Hey day, tirri diddle, hey day!
  [*Sings.*
  Wol. What? Are you singing, sirrah?
  Will. I'll make him cry as fast anon, I hold a penny.
  Dud. Good morrow to your grace, my good lord cardinal.
  Wol. We thank your honour.

        Enter KING *within.*

  King. What! Compton! Carew! [*Calls within.*
  Bran. Hark! the king calls.
  King. Mother of God! How are we attended on! Who waits without?
  Bran. Go in, Sir William! and if you find his grace
In any milder temper than he was last night,
Let us have word, and we will visit him.
  Comp. I will, my lord. [*Exit.*
  Wol. What is the occasion the king's so moved?
  Bran. His grace hath taken such an inward grief
With sad remembrance of the queen that's dead,
That much his highness wrongs his state and person.
Besides in Ireland do the Burkes rebel,
And stout Pearsie, that disclosed the plot,
Was by the Earl of Kildare put to death.
And Martin Luther out of Germany
Has writ a book against his majesty,
For taking part with proud Pope Julius,
Which being spread by him through Christendom,
Hath thus incensed his royal majesty.
  Wol. Tush! I have news, my lord, to salve that sore,
And make the king more feared through Christendom,
Than ever was his famous ancestors:
Nor can base Luther, with his heresies,
Backed by the proudest German potentate,
Heretically blur king Henry's fame,
For honour that he did Pope Julius,
Who, in high favour of his majesty,
Hath sent Campeius with a bull from Rome,

To add unto his title this high stile:
That he and all his fair posterity
Proclaimed Defenders of the Faith shall be;
For which intent the holy cardinal's come
As legate from the imperial court of Rome.

Gray. This news, my lord, may something ease his mind:
'Twere good, your grace would go and visit him.

Wol. I will, and doubt not but to please him well.
[*Exit.*

Sey. So! I am glad he's in: an the king be no better pleased than he was at our last parting, he'll make him repent his sauciness.

Bran. How now, old William? How chance you go not to the king and comfort him?

Will. No, by'r lady, my lord. I was with him too lately already, his fist is too heavy for a fool to stand under. I went to him last night after you had left him, seeing him chafe so at Charles here, to make him merry: and he gave me such a box on the ear, that struck me clean through three chambers, down four pair of stairs; I fell over five barrels into the bottom of the cellar, and if I had not well liquored myself there, I had never lived after it.

Bran. Faith, Will, I'll give thee a velvet coat, an thou canst but make him merry.

Will. Will ye, my lord? and I'll venture another box on the ear, but I'll do it.

Enter COMPTON.

Comp. Clear the presence there; the king is coming.
God's me, my lords, what meant the cardinal,
So unexpected thus to trouble him?

Gray. Is the king moved at it?

Enter the KING *and* WOLSEY.

Comp. Judge by his countenance: see he comes!
Bran. I'll not endure the storm.
Dud. Nor I.
Will. Run fool, your master will be felled else.
King. Did we not charge that none should trouble us?
Presumptuous priest, proud prelate as thou art,
How comes it, you are grown so saucy, sir,
Thus to presume upon our patience,
And cross our royal thought, disturbed and vex'd

By all your negligence in our estate
Of us and of our country's happiness?
  Wol. My gracious lord!
  King.   Thou fawning beast, stand back,
Or by my crown, I'll foot thee to the earth!
Where's Brandon, Surrey, Seymour, Gray?
Where is your council now? O, now ye crouch
And stand like pictures at our presence door.
Call in the guard and bear them to the Tower!
Mother of God! I'll have the traitors' heads.
Go, hail them to the block: up, up, stand up!
I'll make ye know your duties to our state:
Am I a cipher? is my sight grown stale?
Am I not Harry? am I not England's king? Ha!
  Will. So la! Now the watchword's given: nay, an he once cry Ha! ne'er a man in the court dare for his head speak again. Lie close, cousin Patch!
  Patch. I'll not come near him, cousin; he's almost killed me with his countenance.
  King. We have been too familiar, now I see,
And you may dally with our majesty.
Where are my pages there?

      Enter Pages.

  First Page. My lord?
  King. Truss, sirrah! None to put my garter on!
Give me some wine! — Here's stuff at th'other side. —
Proud cardinal, who followed our affairs in Italy,
That we, that honoured so Pope Julius,
By dedicating books, at thy request,
Against that upstart sect of Lutherans,
Should by that heretic be bandied thus?
But by my George I swear, if Henry live,
I'll hunt base Luther through all Germany,
And pull those seven electors on their knees,
If they but back him 'gainst our dignity. —
Base slave, tie soft, thou hurt'st my leg! — [*To the page.*
And now in Ireland the Burkes rebel,
And with their stubborn kerns make hourly roads,
To burn the borders of the English pale:
And which of all your counsels helps us now?

    Enter COMPTON *with wine.*

  Comp. Here's wine, my lord!

King. Drink and be damn'd! — I cry thee mercy, Compton.
What the devil meantst thou to come behind me so?
I did mistake, I'll make thee amends for it.
By holy Paul, I am so crossed and vex'd,
I knew not what I did: and here at home
Such careful statesmen do attend us,
And look so wisely to our common-weal,
That we have ill May-days, and riots made,
For lawless rebels do disturb our state.
Twelve times this term have we in person sat,
Both in the Star-Chamber and Chancery-Courts,
To hear our subjects' suits determined.
Yet 'tis your office, Wolsey: but all of you
May make a packhorse of king Harry now.
Well, what would you say?

Wol. Nothing that might displease your majesty;
I have a message from the pope to you.

King. Then keep it still, we will not hear it yet:
Get all of you away, avoid our presence,
We cannot yet command our patience.

[*Exeunt Wolsey, lords &c.*

Reach me a chair!

Bran. Now, Will, or never! Make the king but smile,
And with thy mirthful toys allay his spleen,
That we, his council, may confer with him,
And by mine honour, I'll reward thee well.
To him, good Will!

Will. Not too fast, I pray, least Will Summers ne'er be seen again: I know his qualities as well as the best on ye, for ever when he's angry, and nobody dare speak to him, ye thrust me in by the head and shoulders, and then we fall to buffets, but I know who has the worst on't: but go, my lord, stand aside, and stir not, till I call ye; let my cousin Patch and I alone, an he go a-boxing, we'll fall both upon him, that's certain: but an the worst come, be sure that the cardinal's fool shall pay for't.

Bran. Use your best skill, good William:
I'll not be seen, unless I see him smile. [*Exit Brandon.*

Will. Where art thou, cousin? Alas, poor fool, he's crept under the table: up, cousin, fear nothing, the storm's past, I warrant thee.

Patch. Is the king gone, cousin?

Will. No, no, yonder he sits: we are all friends now, the

lords are gone to dinner, and thou and I must wait at the king's table.

Patch. Not I, by'r lady, I would not wait upon such a lord for all the livings in the land: I thought he would have killed my lord cardinal, he looked so terribly.

Will. Foh, he did but jest with him; but I'll tell thee, cousin, the rarest trick to be revenged at's passes, and I'll give thee this fine silk point an thou'lt do it.

Patch. O brave, O brave, give me it, cousin, and I'll do whatsoever 'tis.

Will. I'll stand behind the post here, and thou shalt go softly stealing behind him as he sits reading yonder, and when thou comest close to him, cry Bo! and we'll scare him so, he shall not tell where to rest him.

Patch. But will he not be angry?

Will. No, no, for then I'll show myself, and after he sees who 'tis, he'll laugh and be as merry as a mag-pie, and thou'lt be a made man by it, for all the house shall see him hug thee in his arms and dandle thee up and down with hand and foot as thou wert a football.

Patch. O fine! Come, cousin, give me the point first, and I'll roar so loud, that I'll make him believe, that the devil's come.

Will. So do and fear nothing, for an thou wert the devil himself he'll conjure thee, I warrant thee: I would not have such a conjuring for twenty crowns: but when he has made way, I'll make him merry enough, I doubt it not: so now, cousin, look to your coxcomb.

Patch. Bo!

King. Mother of God, what's that?

Patch. Bo!

King. Out ass, and tumble at my feet,
For thus I'll spurn thee up and down the house.

Patch. Help, cousin, help.

Will. No, cousin, now he's conjuring; I dare not come near him.

King. Who set this natural here to trouble me?

Enter COMPTON.

Who's that stands laughing there? The fool! Ha, ha! Where's Compton? Mother o' God, I have found his drift: 'tis the craftiest old villain in Christendom. Mark, good Sir William, because the fool durst not come near himself, seeing our anger, he sent this silly ass, that we might wreak our royal spleen on him, whilst he stands laughing to behold the jest: by th' blessed Lady, Compton, I'll not leave the fool to gain a million, he contents me so. Come hither, Will!

Will. I'd know whether ye have done knocking first: my cousin Patch looks pitifully. Ye had best be friends with us, I can tell you: we'll scare you out of your skin else.

King. Alas, poor Patch: hold, sirrah, there's an angel to buy you points.

Will. La, cousin, did not I say, he'll make much on ye?

Patch. Ay, cousin, but he's made such a singing in my head, I cannot see where I am.

Will. All the better, cousin, an your head fall a singing, your feet may fall a dancing and so save charges to the piper.

King. Will Summers, pr'ythee, tell me why didst thou send him first?

Will. Because I'd have him have the first fruits of thy fury. I knew, how the matter stood with the next that disturbed thee, therefore I kept i' th' rearward, that if the battle grew too hot, I might run presently.

King. But wherefore came ye?

Will. To make thee leave thy melancholy and turn merry man again: thou hast made all the court in such a pitiful case as passes. The lords has attended here this four days and none dares speak to thee, but thou art ready to chop off their heads for it: and now I, seeing what a fretting fury thou continuedst in, and every one said 'twould kill thee if thou keptst it, pulled e'en up my heart and vowed to loose my head, but I'd make thee leave it.

King. Well, William, I am beholding to ye. Ye shall have a new coat and cap for this.

Will. Nay, then I shall have two new coats and caps, for Charles Brandon promised me one before to perform this enterprise.

King. He shall keep his word, Will. Go, call him in, Call in the lords, tell them our spleen is calm'd:
Mother o' God, we must give way to wrath,
That chafes our royal blood with anger thus,
And use some mirth, I see, to comfort us.

Enter BRANDON *and other* LORDS.

Draw near us, lords; Charles Brandon, list to me,

Will Summers here must have a coat of you,
But Patch has earned it dearest: where's the fool?
    Will. He's e'en creeping as near the door as he can; he'd fain be gone, I see, an he could get out. Wouldst thou not, cousin?
    Patch. Yes, cousin Will; I'd fain be walking, I am afraid I am not as I should be.
    Will. Come, I'll help thee out then. Dost thou hear, my lord cardinal, your fool is in a pitiful taking; he smells terribly.
    Wol. You are too crafty for him, William.
    King. So is he, Wolsey, credit me.
    Will. I think so, my lord: as long as Will lives, the cardinal's fool must give way to the king's fool.
    King. Well, Sir, be quiet; and my reverend lords,
I thank you for your patient suffering:
We were disturbed in our thoughts, we swear,
We now entreat you speak, and we will hear.
    Wol. Then may it please your sacred majesty,
Campeius, legate to his holiness,
Attends with letters from the court of Rome.
    King. Let him draw near, we'll give him audience:
Dudley and Gray, attend the cardinal,
And bring Campeius to our presence here.
    Dud. Gray. We go, my lord.   *[Exeunt.*

    Enter CAMPEIUS *with the other Legates, and Lords.*

    King. Brandon and Seymour, place yourselves by us,
To hear this message from his holiness.
You reverend princes, pillars of the church,
Legates apostolic, how fares the pope?
    Cam. In health, great king, and from his sacred lips
I bring a blessing apostolical
To English Henry and his subjects all:
And more to manifest his love to thee,
The prop and pillar of the church's peace,
And gratify thy love, made plain to him
In learned books 'gainst Luther's heresy,
He sends me thus to greet thy majesty,
With stile and titles of high dignity:
Command the heralds and the trumpets forth.
    Sey. Gentlemen, dispatch and call them in.
    Will. Lord bless us, what's here to do now?

Cam. Receive this bull sent from his holiness
For confirmation of this dignity
To thee and to thy fair posterity.
    Will. 'Tis well the king is a widower: an ye had put forth your bull with his horns forward, I'd have marred your message, I can tell ye.
    King. Peace, Will! Heralds, attend him!
    Cam. Trumpets prepare, whilst we aloud pronounce
This sacred message from his holiness,
And in his reverend name I here proclaim,
Henry the Eighth, by the Grace of God,
King of England, France, and Ireland,
And to this title from the pope we give:
Defender of the Faith in peace to live.
    Wol. Sound trumpets, and God save the king!
    King. We thank his holiness for this princely favour,
Receiving it with thanks and reverence,
In which, whilst we have life, his grace shall see,
Our sword Defender of the Faith shall be.
Go one of you, salute the mayor of London,
Bid him with heralds and with trumpets' sound
Proclaim our titles through his government:
Go, Gray, and see it done; attend him, fellows!
    Gray. I go, my lord; trumpets, follow me.   [*Exit.*
    King. What more, lord legate, doth his holiness will?
    Cam. That Henry, joining with the Christian kings
Of France and Spain, Denmark and Portugal,
Would send an army to assail the Turk,
That now invades with war the isle of Rhodes,
Or send twelve thousand pounds to be dispos'd,
As his holiness thinks best, for their relief.
    Will. I thought so; I knew 'twould be a money matter when all's done. Now thou'rt Defender of the Faith, the pope will have thee defend every thing: himself and all.
    King. Take hence the fool.
    Will. Ay, when?, can ye tell? Dost thou think any o'th lords will take the fool? None here, I warrant, except the cardinals.
    King. What a knavish fool's this: lords, you must bear' with him. Come hither, Will: what sayst thou to this new title given us by the pope? Speak, is it not rare?
    Will. I know not how rare it is, but I know how dear

'twill be, for I perceive 'twill cost thee twelve thousand pounds at least, besides the cardinal's cost in coming.

King. All that's nothing; the title of Defender of the Faith is worth ye twice as much: say, is it not?

Will. No, by my troth; dost hear, old Harry, I am sure the true faith is able to defend itself without thee, and as for the pope's faith — good faith! 'tis not worth a farthing, and therefore give him not a penny.

King. Go to, sirrah, meddle not you with the pope's matters!

Will. Let him not meddle with thy matters then: for an he meddle with thee, I'll meddle with him, that's certain, and so farewell. I'll go and meet my little young master, Prince Edward: they say he comes to court to-night: I'll to horse-back, pr'ythee Harry, send one to hold my stirrup. Shall I tell the prince what the pope has done?

King. Ay, an thou wilt, Will; he shall be Defender of the Faith too, one day.

Will. No, an he and I can defend ourselves, we care not, for we are sure the faith can. [*Exit.*

King. Lord legate, so we reverence Rome and you,
As nothing you demand shall be denied:
The Turk will we expel from Christendom,
Sending stout soldiers to his holiness,
And money to relieve distressed Rhodes:
So, if you please, pass in to banqueting.
Go, lords, attend them! Brandon and Compton, stay,
We have some business to confer upon.

Cam. We take our leave. [*Exit.*

King. Most hearty welcome to my reverend lords! —
So now to our business. Brandon, say,
Hear ye no tidings from our sister Mary,
Since her arrival in the realm of France?

Bran. Thus much we heard, my lord: at Calais met her
The youthful Dauphin, and the peers of France,
And bravely brought her to the king at Tours,
Where he both married her and crowned her queen.

King. 'Tis well. Brandon and Compton, list to me,
I must employ your aid and secrecy:
This night we mean in some disguised shape
To visit London and to walk the round,
Pass through their watches and observe the care
And special diligence to keep our peace.

They say, night walkers hourly pass the streets,
Committing theft and hated sacrilege,
And slightly pass unstayed or unpunished.
Go, Compton, go and get me some disguise,
This night we'll see our City's government.
Brandon, do you attend at Baynard's Castle,
Compton shall go disguised along with me,
Our swords and bucklers shall conduct us safe,
But if we catch a knock to quit our pain,
We'll put it up, and hie us home again. [*Exeunt*.

Enter the CONSTABLE *and Watch,* PRICHALL, *the Cobbler, being one, bearing a lantern.*

   Const. Come, neighbours: we have a straight command
Our watches be severely looked into:
Much theft and murder was committed lately.
There are two strangers, merchants of the Stillyard,
Cruelly slain found floating on the Thames,
And greatly are the Stewes had in suspect,
As places fitting for no better use:
Therefore be careful and examine all,
Perhaps we may attach the murderer.
   First Watch. Nay, I assure ye, master constable, those stew houses are places of much slaughter and redemption, and many cruel deeds of equity and wickedness are committed there, for divers good men lose both their money and their computation by them, I abjure ye. How say you, neighbour Prichall?
   Prich. Neighbour Capcase, I know you're a man of courage, and for the merry cobbler of Limestreet, though I sit as low as Saint Faith's, I can look as high as Saint Paul's. I have in my days walked to the Stewes as well as my neighbours, but if the mad wenches fall to murdering once and cast men into the Thames, I have done with them: there's no dealing, if they carry fire in one hand and water i' th' tother.
   Const. Well, masters, we are now placed about the king's business,
And I know ye all sufficient in the knowledge of it,
I need not to repeat your charge again:
Good neighbours, use your greatest care, I pray,
And if unruly persons trouble ye,
Call and I'll come: so, sirs, good night. [*Exit*.
   First Watch. God ye good night and twenty, sir; I warrant ye, ye need not reconcile to our charge, for some one

on us has discharged the place this forty year, I am sure. Neighbours, what think you best to be done?

Prich. Every man according to his calling, neighbour: if the enemy come, here lies my town of garrison, I set on him as I set on a patch: if he tread on this side, I underlay him on this side, or prick him through both sides, I yerk him and trick him, pare him and piece him, then hang him up by th' heels till Sunday.

First Watch. How say ye? By my faith, neighbour Prichall, ye speak to the purpose: for indeed, neighbours, if every man take a nap now i' th' forehand o' th' night and go to bed afterward?

Prich. That were not amiss neither, but an you'll take but every man his pot first, you'll sleep like the man i' th' moon, i' faith.

Sec. Watch. Do ye think, neighbour, there is a man i' th' moon?

First Watch. I assure ye, in a clear day I have seen't at midnight.

Sec. Watch. Of what occupation is he, trow?

Prich. Some thinks he's a shepherd, because on's dog, some says he's a baker going to heat his oven with a bavin at's back; but the plain truth is, I think, he is a cobbler, for ye know what the song says: —

  I see a man i' th' moon,
    Fie, man, fie,
  I see a man i' th' moon,
    Clouting Saint Peter's shoon —

and so by this reason he should be a cobbler.

First Watch. By my fekins, he saith true. Alas, alas, goodman Dormouse hath even given up the ghost already: 'tis an honest quiet soul, I warrant ye.

Prich. It behoves us all to be so. How do ye, neighbour Dormouse?

Dorm. God speed ye, God speed ye! Nay, an ye go a God's name, I have nothing to say to ye.

Sec. Watch. La ye, his mind's on business, though he be ne'er so sleepy.

Prich. Come, let's all join with him and steal a nap, every man, my masters, to his several stall.

Sec. Watch. Agreed; good night, good neighbours.

Prich. Nay, let's take no leave, I'll but wink a-while and see you again.

Enter KING *and* COMPTON *with bills on their backs.*

King. Come, Sir William,
We may now stand upon our guard, you see,
The watch has given us leave to arm ourselves,
They fear no danger, for they sleep secure.
Go, carry those bills we took to Baynard's Castle,
And bid Charles Brandon to disguise himself
And meet me presently at Gracechurch Corner;
We will attempt to pass through all the watches,
And so I take't, 'twill be an easy task:
Therefore make haste.
    Comp. I will, my liege.
    King. The watchword, if I chance to send to ye,
Is, The Great Stag of Baydon — so my name shall be.
    Comp. Enough, we'll think on it.   [*Exit.*
    King. So now we'll forward. Soft, yonder's a light,
Ay, and a watch, and all asleep — by'r lady!
These are good peaceable subjects: here's none
Beckons to any, all may pass in peace.
Ho sirrah!
    Prich.   Stand, who goes there?
    King. A good fellow. 'Stand' is a heinous word i'th' king's highway: you have been at noddy, I see.
    Prich. Ay, and the first card comes to my hand is a knave.
    King. I am a court-card indeed.
    Prich. Then thou must needs be a knave, for thou art neither king nor queen, I am sure; but whither goest thou?
    King. About a little business that I have in hand.
    Prich. Then good night, pr'ythee trouble me no longer.
    King. Why, this is easy enough, here's passage at pleasure,
What wretch so wicked, would not give fair words
After the foulest fact of villany,
That may escape unseen so easily,
Or what should let him, that is so resolv'd,
To murder, rapine, theft, or sacrilege?
I see the City are the sleepy heads
To do it, and pass thus examined.
Fond, heedless men, what boots it for a king
To toil himself in highest state affairs,
To summon parliaments and call together
The wisest heads of all his provinces

For making statutes for his subjects' peace,
That thus neglecting them, their woes increase.
Well, we will further on: soft, here comes one!
I'll stay and see, how he escapes the watch.

Enter BLACK WILL.

Black W. So now I am got within the City, I am as safe as in a sanctuary: it is a hard world, when Black Will for a venture of five pound must commit such petty robberies at Mile End, but the plain truth is, the Stewes from whence I had my quarterage, is now grown too hot for me: there's some suspicion of a murder lately done upon two merchants of the Stillyard, which indeed, as far as some five or six stabs comes to, I confess I had a hand in. But mumbudget, all the dogs in the town must not bark at it. I must withdraw a-while till the heat be o'er, remove my lodging, and live upon dark nights and misty mornings. Now, let me then see the strongest watch in London intercept my passage.

King. [*Aside.*] Such a fellow would I fain meet withal. — Well overtaken, sir.

Black W. 'Sblood! come before me, sir: what the devil art thou?

King. A man at least.

Black W. And art thou valiant?

King. I carry a sword and buckler, ye see.

Black W. A sword and buckler? and know not me, not Black Will?

King. No, trust me.

Black W. Slave, then thou art neither traveller, nor pursetaker, for I tell thee, Black Will is known and feared through the seventeen Provinces: there's not a sword and buckler-man in England, nor Europe, but has had a taste of my manhood. I am toll-free in all cities and the suburbs about them: this is my sconce, my castle, my citadel, and but King Harry, God bless his majesty, I fear not the proudest.

King. O yes, some of his guard.

Black W. Let his guard eat his beef and be thankful: give me a man will cover himself with his buckler and not budge, an the devil come.

King. Methinks, thou wert better live at court, as I do; King Harry loves a man, I can tell you.

Black W. Would thou and all the men he keeps were

4*

hanged, an ye love not him then; but I will not change my revenues for all his guards' wages.

King. Hast thou such store of living?

Black W. Art thou a good fellow? May I speak freely and wilt not tell the king on't?

King. Keep thine own counsel and fear not, for of my faith, the king shall know no more for me than thou tellst him.

Black W. An I tell him any thing, let him hang me: but for thyself, I think, if a fat purse come i' th' way, thou wouldst not refuse it. Therefore leave the court and shark with me; I tell thee I am chief commander of all the Stewes, there's not a whore shifts a smock but by my privilege, nor opens her shop, before I have my weekly tribute: and to assure thee my valour carries credit with it, do but walk with me through the streets of London and let me see the proudest watch disturb us.

King. I shall be glad of your conduct, sir.

Black W. Follow me then, and I'll tell thee more.

First Watch. Stand, who goes there?

Black W. A good fellow. Come close, regard them not!

Sec. Watch. How shall we know thee to be a good fellow?

Black W. My name's Black Will.

First Watch. O, God give ye good night, good master Black William.

Sec. Watch. Good bye, sir, good bye. I am glad, we are so well rid on him.

Black W. La, sir, you see and here's egress enough; now follow me, and you shall see we'll have regress back again.

First Watch. Who comes there?

Prich. Come 'afore the constable!

Black W. What, have ye forgot me so soon? 'Tis I.

Sec. Watch. O, 'tis master Black William: God bless ye, sir, God bless ye.

Black W. How likest thou now?

King. Faith, excellent: but pr'ythee tell me, dost thou face the world with thy manhood, that thus they fear thee, or art thou truly valiant?

Black W. 'Sfoot, dost thou doubt of my manhood? Nay then defend yourself, I'll give you a trial presently: betake ye to your tools, sir, I'll teach ye to stand upon interrogatories.

King. I am for ye, there's ne'er a man the king keeps,

shall refuse ye; but tell me, wilt thou keep the king's act for fighting?

Black W. As ye please, sir; yet because thou'rt his man, I'll observe it and neither thrust nor strike beneath the knee.

King. I am pleased, sir; have at you, sir.   [*They fight.*

First Watch. Help, neighbours! O take ye to your brown bills, call up the constable, here's a piece of chance meddle ready to be committed. Set on, goodman Prichall!

Prich. I'll firk them on both sides: lie close, neighbour Dormouse! Keep the king's peace, I charge ye! Help, master Constable!

Enter the CONSTABLE.

Const. Keep the peace, or strike them down!

Black W. 'Swoons, I am hurt; hold, I say.

Sec. Watch. Let them not pass, neighbours; here's bloodshed drawn upon one of the king's officers.

Const. Take away their weapons, and since you are so hot, I'll set you where you shall be cool enough.

Black W. 'Swoons, the moon's a waning harlot; with the glimpse of her light I lost his point and mistook my ward he'd ne'er broached my blood else.

Const. Pray, sir, what are you?

King. I am the king's man, sir, and of his guard.

Const. More shame you should so much forget yourself, For as I take't, 'tis parcel of your oath,
As well to keep his peace, as guard his person:
And if a constable be not present by,
You may as well as he his place supply:
And seeing ye so neglect your oath and duty,
Go, bear them to the Counter presently;
There shall ye answer for these misdemeanours.

Sec. Watch. He's broke my head, sir, and furthermore it bleeds.

Const. Away with them both, they shall pay thee well, ere they come forth, I warrant thee.

Black W. I beseech ye, sir.

ing. Never entreat, man, we shall have bail, I doubt it not. But, master constable, I hope you'll do me this favour, to let one of your watchmen go of an errand for me, if I pay him.

Const. With all my heart, sir: here's one shall go.

King. Hold thee, good fellow, here's an angel for thee, go thy way to Baynard's Castle and ask for one Brandon — he serves the Duke of Suffolk — and tell him his bedfellow, or the Great Stag of Baydon, this night is clapped i' th' Counter, and bid him come speak with me. Come, constable, let's go: sirrah, make haste. [*Exit.*

Prich. I warrant you, sir, an this be all, I'd have done it for half the money. Well, I must enquire for one Brandon and tell him the Great Stag of Baydon is i' th' Counter. By'r lady, I doubt they be both crafty knaves and this is some watchword between them both: mass, I doubt he ne'er came well by his money, he's so liberal. Well, I'll forward.

Enter BRANDON *and* COMPTON.

Bran. Sir William, are you sure it was at Gracechurch His majesty appointed we should meet him?
We have been there and missed him: what think ye, sir?
Comp. Good faith, I know not.
His highness is too venturous bold, my lord;
I know he will forsake himself in this,
Opposing still against a world of odds.
Bran. Good faith, 'tis true: but soft, here comes one.
How now, good fellow, whither goest thou?
Prich. It lies in my authority, sir, to ask you that question, for I am one of the king's watch, I can tell ye.
Comp. Then perhaps thou canst tell us some tidings: didst thou not see a good, lusty, tall, big man pass through your watches to-night?
Prich. Yes, sir, there was such a man came to our watch to-night, but none that passed through, for he behaved himself so that he was laid on quickly, and now he is forthcoming in the Counter.
Bran. And whither art thou going?
Prich. Faith, sir, he's given me an angel to do an errand for him at Baynard's Castle to one Brandon that serves the Duke of Suffolk; he says, he is his bedfellow, and I must tell him, the Great Stag of Baydon is i' th' Counter.
Bran. If thine errand be to Brandon, I can save thee a labour, for I am the man thou look'st for; we have been seeking him almost all this night: hold thee, there's an angel for thy news, I'll bail him, I warrant thee. [*Exeunt.*
Prich. I thank you, sir, but he's not so soon bailed as

you think, for there's two of the king's watch has their heads broke, and that must be answered for: but all's one to me, let them shuffle as they will, the angels has flown about to-night and two gulls are light into my hands and these I'll keep, let him get out as he can. [*Exit.*

Enter the KING *in prison.*

King. Ho, porter, who's without there?

Port. What's the matter now? will ye not go to bed to-night?

King. No, trust me, 'twill be morning presently,
And I have hope, I shall be bailed ere then:
I pr'ythee, if thou canst, entreat some of the prisoners to keep me company a pair of hours or so, and we'll spend them i' th' rouse of healths, and all shall be my cost. Say, wilt thou pleasure me?

Port. If that will pleasure ye, sir, ye shall not want for company, here's enough that can tend it, they have hunger and ease enough at all times

King. There's a couple of gentlemen in the next room, I pr'ythee let them come in, and there's a Harry sovereign for thee.

Port. I thank you, sir; I am as much beholding to you as to king Harry for it. [*Exit.*

King. Ay, I assure thee, thou art. —
Well, master constable, you've made the Counter
This night the royal court of England's king,
And by my crown I swear, I would not for
A thousand pound 'twere otherwise.
The officers in cities, now I see,
Are like the orchard set with several trees,
Where one must cherish one, rebuke the other,
And in this wretched Counters, I perceive,
Money plays fast and loose, purchases favour,
And without that, nought but misery.
A poor gentleman hath made complaint to me:
'I am undone, quoth he, and kept in prison,
For one of your fellows that serves the king,
Being bound for him and he neglecting me,
Hath brought me to this woe and misery.'
Another citizen there is, complains
Of one belonging to the cardinal,

That in his master's name hath taken up
Commodities, valued at a thousand pound,
The payment being deferr'd, hath caused him break,
And so is quite undone. Thus kings and lords, I see,
Are oft abused by servants' treachery.
But whist a while, here comes my fellow prisoners.

Enter the Prisoners.

First Pris. Where's this bully Grig, this lad of life, that will scour the Counter with right Rhenish to-night? O sir, you are welcome.

King. I thank ye, sir: nay, we'll be as great as our word, I assure ye. Here, porter, there's money, fetch wine, I pr'ythee. Gentlemen, you cannot be merry in this melancholy place, but here's a lad has his heart as light as his purse. Sirrah, thou art some mad slave, I think, a regular companion, one that uses to walk o' nights, or so; art thou not?

First Pris. Hark in thine ear, thou'rt a good fellow.

King. I am right born, I assure thee.

First Pris. King Harry loves a man and thou a woman: Shall I teach thee some wit and tell thee, why I meet thee here? I went and set my lime-twigs and I think, I got some hundred pound by a crooked measure at Coome-Park, and now seeing there was watch laid and much search for suspicious persons, I got one as honest as myself to arrest me by a contrary name and lay me in the Counter, and here I know they'll ne'er seek me, and so when the heat's o'er, I am at liberty and mean to spend my crowns lustily. How lik'st thou this, my bully?

King. An excellent policy.

First Pris. But mum, no words: use't for yourself, or so.

King. O sir, fear it not. Be merry, gentlemen: is not this wine come yet? God's me, forgot our chief guest: where's my sword and buckler-man? Where's Black Will? How now, man? melancholy? Let not a little wipe make us enemies, clap hands and be friends.

Black W. My blood's up still.

King. When 'tis at highest, 'twill fall again; come, hands, hands.

Black W. I'll shake hands with thee, because thou carriest a sword and buckler, yet thou'rt no right cavalier, thou knowst not how to use them, thou hast a heavy arm.

King. Ay, a good smart stroke.

Black W. Thou cutst my head indeed, but 'twas no play, thou layst open enough, I could have entered at my pleasure.

King. Nay, I have stout guard, I assure ye.

Black W. Childish to a man of valour: when thou shouldst have born thy buckler here, thou letst it fall to thy knee; thou gavest me a wipe, but 'twas mere chance: but had we not been parted, I had taught ye a little school-play, I warrant ye.

Bran. [*speaks within*]. What ho, porter! who keeps the gates there?

Port. Who knocks so fast?

Enter BRANDON *and* COMPTON *hastily.*

Comp. Stand by, sirrah

Port. Keep back, I say: whither will ye press amongst the prisoners?

Bran. Sirrah, to the court, and we must in.

Port. Why, sir, the court's not kept i'th' Counter to-day.

Bran. Yes, when the king is there.
All happiness betide our sovereign!

Black W. 'Swoons, King Harry.

First Pris. Lord, I beseech thee, no.

Omnes. We all entreat your grace to pardon us.

King. Stand up, good men: beshrew you, Brandon, for discovering us, we shall not spend our time so well this month: but there's no remedy now, the worst is this, the court, good fellows, must be removed the sooner. Ye all are courtiers yet. Nay, nay, come forward,   [*To first Prisoner.*
Even now, you know, we were more familiar:
You see policies holds not always current,
I am found out, and so, I think, will you be.
Go, porter, let him be removed to Newgate,
This place, I see, is too secure for him:
We'll send you further word for his bestowing.

First Pris. I beseech your grace.

King. There is no grace in thee, nor none for thee: Away with him.   [*Exeunt Porter and Prisoners.*

Black W. 'Swoons, I shall to Tyburn presently.

King. The gentlemen, that have been wronged by
My servants and the cardinal's shall give
Me nearer notes of it,
Both what they are, and how much debt they owe ye.
Send your petitions to the court to me,
And doubt not but you shall have remedy;
There's forty angels, drink to king Harry's health,
And think withal, much wrong king's men may do,
The which their masters ne'er consent unto.

Sec. Pris. God bless your majesty with happy life,
That thus respects your woful subjects' grief.

King. Where's Black Will? Nay, come nearer, man: I came nearer you, though ye misliked my play.

Black W. By th' Lord, your majesty's the best sword and buckler-man in Europe: ye lie as close to your wards, carry your point as fair, that no fencer comes near ye for gallant fence play.

King. Nay, now ye flatter me.

Black W. 'Fore God, ye broke my head most gallantly.

King. Ay, but 'twas by chance, ye know; but now your head's broke, you look for a plaster, I am sure.

Black W. An your grace will give me leave, I'll put it up and go my ways presently.

King. Nay, soft, sir: the keeper will deny ye that privilege. Come hither, sirrah: because ye shall know King Harry loves a man and I perceive there's some mettle in thee, there's twenty angels for thee. Marry, it shall be to keep ye in prison still, till we have further use for ye. If ye can break through watches with egress and regress so valiantly, ye shall do't amongst your country's enemies.

Black W. The wars, sweet king, 'tis my delight, my desire, my chair of state; create me but a tattered corporal, and give me some pre-eminence over the vulgar hot-shots: an I beat them not forward to as brave attempts and march myself i' th' vanguard, as e'er cannon against a castle wall, break my head in two places more and consume me with the mouth of a double culverin: I'll live and die with thee, sweet king.

King. 'Twill be your best course, sir: go, take him in, When we have need of men, we'll send for him.

Black W. God bless your majesty: I'll go drink to your health. [*Exit.*

King. Be gone, sir: keeper, I thank you for your lodging;
Nay, indeed, I do; I know, had ye known us, it had been better;
Pray, tell the constable that brought us hither,
We thank him and commend his faithful service.
Gentlemen, let's hear from you, and so good morrow.
Keeper, there's for my fees, discharge the officers,
And give them charge that none discover us,.
Till we are past the city· in this disguise we came,
We'll keep us still, and so depart again.
Once more, good morrow; you may now report,
Your Counter was one night king Henry's court.
Away, and leave us. [*Exit Keeper.*] Brandon, what further news?

Bran. The old king of France is dead, my liege,
And left your sister Mary a young widow.

King. God forbid, man! What, not so soon, I hope,
She has not yet been married forty days:
Is this news certain?

Bran. Most true, my lord.

King. Alas, poor Mary, so soon a widow,
Before thy wedding-robes be half worn out?
We must then prepare black funeral garments too:
Well, we will have her home, the league is broke,
And we'll not trust her safety to the French.
Charles Brandon, you shall go to France for her;
See that your train be richly furnished,
And if the daring French brave thee in attempts
Of honour, barriers, tilt, and tournament,
So to retain her, bear thee like thyself,
An English man, dreadless of the proudest,
And highly scorning lowly hardiness.

Bran. I shall, my sovereign, and in her honour
I'll cast a challenge through all the court,
And dare the proudest peer in France for her.

King. Commend me to the Lady Katherine Parr,
Give her this ring, tell her on Sunday next
She shall be queen and crown'd at Westminster,
And Anne of Cleve shall be sent home again.
Come, sirs, we'll leave the City and the Counter now·
The day begins to break, let's hie to court,
And once a quarter we desire such sport. [*Exeunt.*

Enter the CARDINAL, *reading a letter,* BONNER *in his bishop's robes.*

Wol. My reverend lord of London,
Our trusty friend, the king of France, is dead,
And in his death our hopes are hindered:
The emperor too mislikes his praises, but
We shall cross him for it, I doubt it not,
And tread upon his pomp imperial,
That thus hath wrong'd the English cardinal.

Bon. Your grace's letters, by Campeius sent,
I doubt not but shall work your full content.

Wol. Ay, that must be our safest way to work,
Money will make us men, when men stand out:
The bastard Frederick, to attain the place,
Hath made an offer to the cardinals
Of threescore thousand pound, which we will pay
Three times thrice double, ere we lose the day.

Enter WILL SUMMERS *and* PATCH.

Patch. Come, cousin William, I'll bring ye to my lord cardinal presently.

Will. I thank ye, cousin, and when you come to the court I'll bring you to the king again; ye know, cousin, he gave ye an angel.

Patch. Ay, but he gave me such a blow o' th' ear for it, as I care not for coming in's sight again while I live.

Wol. How now, Patch? who have you got there? What? Will Summers? Welcome, good William.

Will. I thank your grace; I heard say, your lordship had made two new lords here, and so the two old fools are come to wait on them.

Bon. We thank ye, William.

Patch. Your lordship will be well guarded, an we follow ye, the king's fool and the cardinal's, and we are no small fools, I assure ye.

Will. No, indeed, my cousin Patch here is something too square to be set on your shoe, marry an you'll wear him on your shoulder, the fool shall ride you.

Wol. A shrewd fool, Bonner: come hither, William, I have a quarrel to you since our last rhyming.

Will. About your fair leman at Charlton, my lord; I remember.

Bon. You speak plain, William.

Will. Ye never knew fool a flatterer, I warrant ye.

Wol. Well, Will, I'll try your rhyming wits once more: what say you to this: —

    The bells hang high,
    And loud they cry,
    What do they speak?

Will.   If you should die,
    There's none would cry,
    Though your neck should break.

Wol. You are something bitter, William; but come on once more, I am for ye: —

    A rod in school,
    A whip for a fool,
    Is always in season.

Will.   A halter and a rope
    For him that would be pope
    Against all right and reason.

Wol. He is too hard for me still, I'll give him over; Come, tell me, Will, what's the news at court?

Will. Marry, my lord, they say the king must be married this morning.

Wol. Married, Will? To whom, I pr'ythee?

Will. Why, to my lady Katherine Parr: I was once by, when he was wooing on her, and then I doubted they would go together shortly.

Wol. Holy Saint Peter shield his majesty,
She is the hope of Luther's heresy:
If she be queen, the protestants will swell,
And Cranmer, tutor to the prince of Wales,
Will boldly speak 'gainst Rome's religion.
But, bishops, we'll to court immediately,
And plot the downfall of these Lutherans.
You two are tutors to the princess Mary,
Still ply her to the pope's obedience,
And make her hate the name of protestant.
I do suspect that Latimer and Ridley,
Chief teachers of the fair Elizabeth,
Are not sound catholics, nor friends to Rome;
If it be so, we'll soon remove them all,

'Tis better, they should die, than thousands fall.
Come, follow us.   [*Exeunt; manent Will and Patch.*

Will. Your lord's mad, till he be at the wedding; 'twas marvel the king stole it so secretly and ne'er told him on't, but all's one: if he be married, let him play with his queen to-night, and then to-morrow he'll call for me; there's no fool to the wilful still. What shall we do, cousin?

Patch. I'll go get the key of the wine-cellar, and thou and I will keep a passage there to-night.

Will. We have but a little wit between us already cousin, and so we should have none at all.

Patch. When our wits be gone, we'll sleep i' th' cellar and lie without our wits for one night.

Will. Content, and then i' th' morning we'll but wet them with another cup more, and they'll shave like a razor all day after. Come close, good coz, let nobody go with us, least they be drunk before us, for fools are innocents and must be accessory to no man's overthrow.   [*Exeunt.*

Sound trumpets. Enter KING, QUEEN KATHERINE, CARDINAL, SEYMOUR, DUDLEY, GRAY. — *Enter* COMPTON *crying 'Hautboys!'*

King. Welcome, queen Katherine, seat thee by our side.
Thy sight, fair queen, by us thus dignified,
Earls, barons, knights, and gentlemen,
Against ye all, we'll be chief challenger,
To fight at barriers, tilt, and tournament,
In honour of the fair queen Katherine.

Q. Kath. We thank your highness and beseech your grace,
Forbear such hazard of your royal person;
Without such honours is your handmaid pleased
Obediently to yield all love and duty,
That may beseem your sacred majesty.

King. God ha' mercy, but where are our children?
Prince Edward, Mary, and Elizabeth,
The royal issue of three famous queens?
How haps we have not seen them here to-day?

Dud. They all, my liege, attend your majesty
And your fair queen within the presence here.

King. 'Tis well, Dudley: call Cranmer in,
He is chief tutor to our princely son,
For precepts that concerns divinity.

Enter CRANMER.

And here he comes. Cranmer, you must ply the prince;
Let his waste hours be spent in getting learning,
And let those linguists for choice languages
Be careful for him in their best endeavours:
Bid doctor Tye ply him to music hard,
He's apt to learn, therefore be diligent,
He may requite your love when we are gone.
 Cran. Our care and duty shall be had, my lord.
 King. We thank ye.
I tell thee, Cranmer, he is all our hopes,
That what our age shall leave unfinished,
In his fair reign shall be accomplished.
Go and attend him!

Enter WILL SUMMERS.

How now, Will Summers, what's the news with you?
 Will. I come to bid thee and thy new queen good morrow.
Look to him, Kate, least he cozen thee, provide civil oranges
enough, or he'll have a lemon shortly.
 Q. Kath. God ha' mercy, Will, thou'lt tell me then, wilt
thou not?
 Will Ay, and watch him too, or let him ne'er trust me:
but dost hear Harry, because I'd have thee have the poor's
prayers, I have brought thee some petitions. The friars and
priests pray too; but I think, 'tis as children say grace, more
for fashion than devotion, therefore the poor's prayers ought
to be soonest heard, because they beg for God's sake; therefore, I pr'ythee, dispatch them.
 King. Read them, Seymour.
 Sey. The humble petition of the Lady Seaton for her
distressed son, that hath in his own defence unhappily slain
a man.
 King. The Lady Seaton? God's holy mother,
Her son has had our pardon twice already,
For two stout subjects that his hand hath slain.
 Will. An any had said so but thou, Harry, I'd have told
him he lied: he ne'er killed but one, thou killedst the t'other;
for an thou hadst hanged him for the first, the two last had
been alive still.
 King. The fool tells true; they wrong our majesty,
That seek our pardon for such cruelty:
Away with it.
 Will. Give me it again, it shall ne'er be seen more, I

assure ye: an I had known, 't had come for that purpose, it should ne'er have been brought for Will, I warrant ye.

Sey. This other comes from two poor prisoners i' th' Counter.

King. We know the inside then, come give them me: Lord cardinal, here's one is dedicated to you.
Hold, read it. Who's there? Compton, enquire for Rokesby, A groom of the wardrobe, and bring him hither.

Comp. I will.

King. Cardinal, what find ye written there?

Wol. Mine own discredit, and th' undoing of An honest citizen by a false servant.

Will. 'Tis not your fool, my lord, I warrant ye.

Wol. No, Will.

Will. I thought so, I knew 'twas one of your knaves, for your fools are harmless.

Q. Kath. Well said, Will, thou lovest thy master's credit, I know.

Will. Ay, Kate, as well as any courtier he keeps: I had rather he should have the poor's prayers, than the pope's.

Q. Kath. Faith, I am of thy mind, Will: I think so too.

King. Take heed what ye say, Kate! What, a Lutheran?

Wol. 'Tis heresy, fair queen, to think such thoughts.

Q. Kath. And much uncharity to wrong the poor.

Will. Well, and when the pope is at best, he is but Saint Peter's deputy, but the poor present Christ and therefore should be something better regarded.

King. Go to, fool.

Wol. Sirrah, you'll be whipped for this.

Will. Would the king would whip thee and all the pope's whelps out of England once, for between ye, ye have racked and pulled it so, we shall be all poor shortly: you have had four hundred threescore pound within this three year for smoke pence: you have smoked it i'faith. Dost hear, Harry, next time they gather them, we have clay enough to make brick, though we want silver mines to make money.

King. Well, William, your tongue is privileged.

Wol. But, my good liege, I fear there's shrewder heads, Although kept close, has set this fool a-work, Thus to extirp against his holiness.

Will. Do not you think so, my lord, nor stomach nobody about it: ye know, what the old proverb says, therefore be patient:
Great quarrellers small credit wins,
When fools set stools, and wise men break their shins.

Therefore think not on it, for I'll sit down by thee, Kate, and say nothing, for here comes one to be examined.

Enter COMPTON *and* ROKESBY.

King. O sir, you're welcome; is your name Rokesby?
Rok. Your poor servant is so called, my lord.
King. Our servant we guess ye by the cloth ye wear, but for your poverty, 'tis doubtful, your credit is so good. Let's see, what's the man's name? Ha, Hopkins! Do you know the man?
Rok. Hopkins? No, my lord.
King. Had you never no dealings with such a man?
Rok. No, if it like your majesty.
King. No, if it like our Majesty! Saucy varlet!
It likes not our majesty, thou shouldst say 'No':
It likes us not, thou liest for that we know.
You know him not, but he too well knows you,
And lies imprisoned, slave, for what's thy due.
Rok. Surely some envious man hath misinform'd.
King. Dar'st thou deny it still, outfacing knave?
Mother o' God, I'll hang thee presently.
Sirrah, ye lie! and though ye wear the king's cloth,
Yet we dare tell ye so before the king:
Slave, thou dost know him.
He here complains, he is undone by thee,
And the king's man hath caused his misery.
Yet you'll outface it still, deny, forswear, and lie, sir? Ha!
Will. Not a word more, if thou lovest thy life, unless thou'lt confess all and speak fair.
Rok. I do beseech your grace.
King. Out, perjur'd knave! What! dost thou serve the king,
And dar'st thou thus abuse our majesty,
And wrong my subjects by thy treachery?
Think'st thou, false thief, thou shalt be privileg'd,
Because thou art my man, to hurt my people?
Villain, those that guard me, shall regard my honour:
Put off that coat of proof, that strong security,
Under which ye march like a halberdier,
Passing through purgatory and none dare strike;
A sergeant's mace must not presume to touch
Your sacred shoulders with the king's own writ.
God's dear lady, does the cloth ye wear,

5

Such privilege and strong prevention bear?
Ha! is it, Rokesby?

Enter a MESSENGER *in haste.*

Mess. My royal lord —
King. Take that and know your time to tell message, sirrah: I am busy.
Will. So there's one served: I think you would take two more with all your heart, so you were well rid on him.
Rok. Your pardon, good my liege.
King. Ha! pardon thee? I tell thee, did it touch
Thy life in ought more than mine own displeasure,
Not all the world should purchase it, vild caitiff:
Hadst thou neglected this thy duty to our person's danger,
Hadst thou thyself against me ought attempted,
I might be sooner won to pardon thee,
Than for a subject's hateful injury.
Q. Kath. Let me entreat your grace to pardon him.
King. Away, Kate, speak not for him!
Out of my lenity I let him live.
Discharge him from my cloth and countenance,
To the Counter to redeem his creditor,
Where he shall satisfy the utmost mite
Of any debt, default, or hinderance:
I'll keep no man to blur my credit so,
My cloth shall not pay what my servants owe.
Away with him!   [*Exit Rokesby.*
Now, my lord cardinal, speaks not your paper so?
Wol. Yes, my good lord, your grace has shown a pattern
To draw forth mine by, I assure your highness.
The punishment inflicted on your man,
Is for my servants meant, that bears such minds,
Their masters thus but serve them in their kinds.
King. Where is this fellow now, that brings us news?
Will. He is gone with a flea in his ear, but has left his message behind him with my lord Dudley here.
King. And what's the news?
Dud.   Duke Brandon, good my liege,—
King. O, he's returned from France; and who comes
                    with him?
Dud. His royal wife, my lord.
King.   Ha! Royal wife! who's that?
Dud. Your highness' sister, the late queen of France.

King. Our sister queen his wife? who gave him her?
Gray. 'Tis said, my liege, they were married at Dover.
King. 'Twere better, he had never seen the town.
Dares any subject mix his blood with ours
Without our leave?

Enter BRANDON *and* LADY MARY.

Dud. He comes himself, my liege, to answer it.
Bran. Health to my sovereign!
King. And our brother king!
Your message is before ye, sir! Off with his head!
Bran. I beseech your grace, give me leave!
King. Nay, you have taken leave! Away with him!
Bid the captain of our guard convey him to the Tower!
Bran. Hear me, my lord.
King. Audacious Brandon, thinkst thou, excuse shall serve?
L. Mary. Right gracious lord!
King. Go to, your prayers will scarce save yourself:
Durst ye contract yourself without our knowledge?
Hence with the hare-brained duke: to the Tower, I say,
And bear our careless sister to the Fleet:
I know, sir, that you broke a lance for her,
And bravely did unhorse the challengers:
Yet was there no such prize set on her head,
That you without our leave should marry her.
Q. Kath. O, good my lord, let me entreat for them.
King. [*Aside.*] Tut, Kate!
Though thus I seem awhile to threaten them,
I mean not to disgrace my sister so.—
Away with them. What say ye, reverend lords,
Is he not worthy of death for his misdeed?
Bon. & Gar. Unless your grace shall please to pardon him.
King. He deserves it then?
Bon. & Gar. He does, my liege.
King. You are knaves and fools and ye flatter me:
God's holy mother! I'll not have him hurt, for all your heads.
Dear Brandon, I embrace thee in mine arms,
Kind sister, I do love you both so well,
I cannot dart another angry frown
To gain a kingdom: here take him, Mary,
I hold thee happier in this English choice,
Than to be queen of France: Charles, love her well!
Now tell on, Brandon, what's the news in France?

5*

Bran. The league is broke betwixt the emperor
And the young king of France; forces are must'ring
On either part, my lord, for horse and foot.
Hot variance is expected speedily,
The emperor is marching now to Landersey
There to invade the towns of Burgundy.
   King. God and Saint George! we'll meet his majesty,
And strike a league of Christian amity.
Lord cardinal, you shall to France with speed,
And in our name salute the emperor;
We'll give direction for your embassage.
The next fair wind shall make us France to greet,
Where Charles the Emperor and the king shall meet.
                                                  [*Exeunt omnes.*

       Enter CRANMER, DOCTOR TYE, *and young* BROWNE *meets them
                 with the Prince's cloak and hat.*

   Cran. How now, young Browne, what have you there?
   Browne. The prince's cloak and hat, my lord.
   Cran. Where is his grace?
   Browne. At tennis, with the marquess Dorset.
   Cran. You and the marquess draw the prince's mind
To follow pleasure and neglect his book,
For which the king blames us. But credit me,
You shall be soundly paid immediately.
   Browne. I pray ye, good my lord, I'll go and call
The prince away.
   Cran. Nay, now ye shall not: who's within there? Ho!

                      Enter Servant.

   Serv. My lord!
   Cran. Go bear this youngster to the chapel straight,
And bid the master of the children whip him well:
The prince, sir, will not learn, and you shall smart for it.
   Browne. O, good my lord, I'll make him ply his book
                       to-morrow.
   Cran. That shall not serve your turn; away, I say.
                                        [*Exit Browne.*
So, sir, this policy was well devised:
Since he was whipped thus for the prince's faults,
His grace hath got more knowledge in a month,
Than he attained in a year before,
For still the fearful boy, to save his breech,

Doth hourly haunt him, wheresoe'er he goes.

Tye.   'Tis true, my lord, and now the prince perceives it,
As loth to see him punish'd for his faults,
Plies it of purpose to redeem the boy:
But pray, my lord, let's stand aside awhile,
And note the greeting 'twixt the prince and him.

Cran.   See where the boy comes, and the king's fool with him;
Let's not be seen, but list their conference.   [*Exeunt.*

Re-enter young BROWNE *with* WILL SUMMERS.

Will.   Nay, boy, an ye cry, you'll spoil your eye-sight: come, come, truss up your hose, you must hold fast your wind, both before and behind, and blow your nose.

Browne.   For what, fool?

Will.   Why, for the mote in thine eye; is there not one in't? wherefore dost thou cry else?

Browne.   I pr'ythee, Will, go call the prince from the tennis-court.

Will.   Dost thou cry for that? nay, then I smell a rat: the prince has played the truant to-day, and his tutors has drawn blood of thy buttocks for't. Why, boy, 'tis honourable to be whipped for a prince.

Browne.   I would, he would either leave the tennis-court and ply his book, or give me leave to be no courtier.

Will.   Ay, for I'll be sworn thy breech lies in the hazard about it, but look, little Ned, yonder he comes.

Enter the PRINCE *and the young* MARQUESS, *with their rackets, divers attending.*

Marq.   Some rubbers for the prince!

Serv.   Here, my good lord.

Prince.   One take our rackets and reach me my cloak:
By my faith, marquess, you are too hard for me.

Marq.   Your grace will say so, though ye over-match me.

Prince.   Why, how now, Browne? what's the matter?

Browne.   Your grace loiters and will not ply your book, and your tutors has whipped me for it.

Prince.   Alas, poor Ned, I am sorry for it, I'll take the more pains and entreat my tutors for thee: yet, in truth, the lectures they read me last night out of Virgil and Ovid, I am perfect in; only I confess, I am something behind in my Greek authors.

Will. And for that speech they have declined it upon his breech.

Prince. And for my logic, thou shalt witness thyself, I am perfect: for now will I prove that, though thou wert whipped for me, yet this whipping was good for thee.

Browne. I'll hardly believe you, my lord, though Ramus himself should prove it: well, *proba*.

Prince. Mark my problem. *Bona virga facit bonum puerum: bonum est, te esse bonum puerum, ergo bona virga res bona est.* And that's this, Ned:—A good rod makes a good boy: 'tis good that thou shouldst be a good boy, therefore a good rod is good.

Will. Nay, by'r lady, the better the rod is, 'tis the worse for him, that's certain: but dost hear me, boy? since he can prove a rod to be so good, let him take't himself the next time.

Prince. In truth, I pity thee and inwardly I feel the stripes thou barest, and for thy sake, Ned, I'll ply my book the faster: in the mean time thou shalt not say but the Prince of Wales will honourably reward thy service; come, Browne, kneel down.

Will. What, wilt thou knight him, Ned?

Prince. I will: my father has knighted many a one, that never shed drop of blood for him, but he has often for me.

Will. O brave! he looks like the Mirror of Knighthood already.

Enter COMPTON.

Comp. Clear the presence, gentlemen, the king is coming.

Prince. The king? God's me, reach me my book, call my tutors in: come, Browne, I'll confirm thy knighthood afore the king.

Marq. Here be your tutors, my lord, and yonder the king comes.

Enter the KING.

Prince. Health to your majesty.

King. God ha' mercy, Ned! Ay, at your book so hard? 'ti, well, 'tis well! Now, bishop Cranmer, and good doctor Tyes I was going to the gallery and to have had your scholar with me, but seeing you're so busy, I'll not trouble him. Come on, Will, come! go you along with me, what make you among the scholars here?

Will. I come to learn my *qui, quae, quod,* to keep me from the rod: marry, here's one was whipped in pudding time, for he has gotten a knighthood about it. Look, old Harry, does he not look more furious than he was wont?

King. Who, Will? young Browne? God's Mary mother! his father is a gallant knight, as any these south parts of England holds.

Will. He cannot compare with his son, though: if he were right Donzel del Phebo, or the very knight of the Sun himself, yet this knight shall unhorse him.

King. When was he made a knight, Will?

Will. Marry, i' th' last action: I can assure you, there was hot service, and some on 'em came so near him, they had like to smell on't: but when all was done, the poor gentleman was pitifully wounded in the back parts, as may appear by the scar, if his knightship would but untruss there.

King. But who knighted him, William?

Will. That did Ned here: and he has earned it too, for I am sure, this two year he has been lashed for his learning.

King. Ha, how? Come hither, Ned; is this true?

Prince. It is, my lord, and I hope your highness will confirm my deed.

King. Confirm it? God's holy mother, what shrewd boys are these!
Cranmer and Tye, do ye observe the prince?
Now, by my crown, young Ned, thou'st honoured me:
I like thy kingly spirit that loves to see
Thy friends advanced to types of dignity.
Young knight, come hither! what the prince hath done
We here confirm: be still Sir Edward Browne!
But hear me, Ned, now you have made him knight,
You must give him some living, or else 'tis nothing.

Will. Ay, by my troth, he is now but a knight under *forma pauperis,* for a knight without living is no better than an ordinary gallant.

King. Well, what will ye give him, Ned?

Prince. When I have heard of something that may do him good, I will entreat your majesty for him, and i' th' mean time from mine own allowance I'll maintain him

King. 'Tis well said; but for your sake, son Edward, we'll provide for him: Cranmer, see presently a patent drawn, wherein we will confirm to him from our Exchequer a thousand marks a year.

Browne. I thank your majesty, and as I am True knight, I'll fight and die for ye.

Will. Now if your tutors come to whip ye, you may choose whether you'll untruss by th' order of arms.

King. Well, Ned, see ye ply your learning and let's have no more knights made in this action: look to him, Browne, if he loiter, his tutors will have you up for't.

Browne. I hope, my lord, they dare not whip me now.

King. By'r lady, sir, that's doubtful.

Will. If they do, he shall make thee a lord, and then they dare not.

King. Well, Cranmer, we'll leave ye: when your pupil has done his task ye set him now, let him come and visit us. On, gentlemen, into the gallery.

Prince. Heaven keep your majesty.   [*Exit King.* Gentlemen, draw near.

Tye. Good morrow to your grace.

Prince. Good morrow, tutors, at noon: 'tis good even, is it not?

Cran. We saw not your grace to-day.

Prince. O ye quip me cunningly for my truantship, that I was not at my book to-day, but I have thought of that ye read last night, I assure ye.

Cran. We doubt it not, fair prince: lords and gentlemen, give leave.

Will. All void the room, there's but scholars and fools.

Cran. I hope, your excellence can answer me in that axiom of philosophy, I propounded to ye.

Prince. I promise ye, tutor, 'tis a problem to me, for the difference of your author's opinions makes me differ in mine own: some say '*Omne animal est aut homo, aut bestia*', that every living creature is or man, or beast.

Will. Then a woman's a beast, for she's no man.

Prince. Peace, William, you'll be expulsed else: and again some authors affirm, that every beast is four-footed.

Will. Then a fool's no beast, for he has but two.

Prince. Yet again, Will?

Will. Mum, Ned, no words, I'll be as still as a small bagpipe.

Cran. *Omne animal est aut homo, aut bestia;* and thus 'tis proved, my lord: *omne animal est rationale, vel irrationale; homo est rationalis, bestia irrationalis; ergo omne animal homo est, vel bestia.*

'Mongst all the creatures in this universe,
Or on the earth, or flying in the air,
Man only reason hath, others only sense;
So what is only sensual, is not man,
But beast: for man both sense and reason hath.
So every creature, having one of these,
Is sure or man or beast, and so all beasts
Are not four-footed.
  Will. That's certain, a louse has six.
  Cran. I beseech your grace.
  Prince. Away, William.
  Will. Not a word more, as I am William.
  Cran. For many beasts have wings, serving instead of feet,
And some have horns, of which we thus esteem:
Animal cornutum non habet dentes supremos,
No horned beast hath teeth above the roof.
  Will. That's a lie, a cuckold has.
  Prince. Thrust the fool out of the presence there.
  Will. Well, *cedant arma togæ,* the scholars shall have the
fool's place.   [*Exit Will.*
  Prince. Well, Cranmer, you have made me able to prove
a man no beast, if he prove not himself so: we'll now leave this.
And now resolve me for divinity;
Cranmer, I love ye and I love your learning;
Speak, and we'll hear ye.
God give ye truth that you may give it me.
This land, ye know, stands wavering in her faith
Betwixt the papists and the protestants.
You know we all must die and this flesh
Part with her part of immortality.
Tutor, I do believe both Heaven and Hell,
Do you know any third place for the soul's abode,
Called purgatory, as some would have me think?
For from my sister Mary and her tutors
I've oft received letters to that purpose.
I love ye, Cranmer, and shall believe whate'er
Ye speak; therefore I charge ye, tell the truth.
  Cran. How thinks your grace, is there a place
Of purgatory, or no?
  Prince.   Truly, I think none,
Yet must I urge to you what's said to me.
This world, you know, hath been five thousand years
Still increasing, still decreasing, still replenish'd,

How long 'twill be, noue knows but he that made it.
We all do call ourselves God's children,
Yet sure some an't: but think ye, tutor, that
The compass of that heaven and hell
Is able to contain those souls so numberless,
That ever breathed since the first breath was given,
Without a *Tertium*, or a third place?
  Cran. Who puts these doubts within your grace's head,
Are like their own belief, slight and unregarded,
And is as easily answer'd and confuted.
Quod est infinitum, non habet finem; cœlum est opus Dei, opus Dei est infinitum: ergo cœlum est infinitum.
That which is infinite hath no end at all,
For that eternity, that everlasting essence,
That did concord heaven, earth, and hell to be,
Is of himself all infinite: that heaven and hell are so,
His power, his works, and words do witness it,
For what is infinite, hath in itself no end.
Then must the heavens which is his glorious seat,
Be incomprehensible containing him,
Then what should need a third place to contain
A world of infinites so vast and main?
  Prince. I thank ye, Cranmer, and I do believe ye.
What other proofs have been maintained to me,
Or shall be, you shall know and aid me in them:
Enough for this time.
Who's there? Doctor Tye, our music lecturer? Pray, draw
near: indeed, I take much delight in ye.
  Tye. In music may your grace ever delight,
Though not in me: music is fit for kings,
And not for those knows not the chime of strings.
  Prince. Truly I love it, yet there are a sort,
Seeming more pure than wise, that will upbraid at it,
Calling it idle, vain, and frivolous.
  Tye. Your grace hath said, indeed they do upbraid
That term is so, and those that do are such
As in themselves no happy concords hold:
All music jars with them, but sounds of good.
But would your grace awhile be patient,
In music's praise, thus will I better it.
Music is heavenly, for in heaven is music,
For there the Seraphins do sing continually,
And when the best was born, that e'er was man,

A quire of angels saug for joy of it;
What of celestial was revealed to man,
Was much of music; 'tis said the beasts did worship,
And sang before the Deity supernal:
The kingly prophet sang before the ark,
And with his music charmed the heart of Saul,
And if the poet fail us not, my lord,
The dulcet tongue of music made the stones
To move, irrational beasts and birds to dance;
And last, the trumpet's music shall awake the dead,
And clothe their naked bones in coats of flesh,
To appear in that high house of parliament,
When those that gnash their teeth at music's sound,
Shall make that place where music ne'er was found.
   Prince. Thou giv'st it perfect life, skilful doctor,
I thank thee for the honour'd praise thou giv'st it;
I pray thee, let us hear it too.
   Tye. 'Tis ready for your grace:
Give breath to your loud-tuned instruments.

Loud Music.

   Prince. 'T is well. Methinks in this sound I prove a
                    complete age;
As music, so is man governed by stops,
Awed by dividing notes, sometimes aloft,
Sometimes below, and when he has attain'd
His high and lofty pitch, breathed his sharpest,
Most shrillest air, yet at length 'tis gone,
And falls down flat to his conclusion.

Soft Music.

Another sweetness and harmonious sound,
A milder strain, another kind agreement:
Yet 'mongst these many strings be one untun'd,
Or jarreth low, or higher than his course,
Not keeping steady mean amongst the rest,
Corrupts them all—so doth bad men the best.
   Tye. Euongh! Let voices now delight his princely ear!

A Song.

   Prince. Doctor, I thank you and commend your cunning.
I oft have heard my father merrily speak
In your high praise, and thus his highness saith:

England one God, one truth, one doctor hath
For music's art, and that is doctor Tye,
Admir'd for skill in music's harmony.
 Tye. Your grace doth honour me with kind acceptance,
Yet one thing more I do beseech your excellence
To deign, to patronize this homely work,
Which I unto your grace have dedicate.
 Prince. What is the title?
 Tye. The Acts of the Holy Apostles turn'd into verse,
Which I have set in several parts to sing,
Worthy Acts and worthily in you remember'd.
 Prince. I'll peruse them and satisfy your pains,
And have them sung within my father's chapel.
I thank ye both. Now I'll crave leave awhile
To be a little idle: pray, let our linguists,
French and Italian, to-morrow morn be ready;
I must confer with them, or I shall lose
My little practise: so good den, good tutors.   [*Exit.*
 Cran. Health to your highness, God increase your days:
The hope of England and of learning's praise.
             [*Exeunt omnes.*

    Enter BONNER *and* GARDINER *reading.*

 Bon. What have you here, my lord of Winchester?
 Gar. Heretical and damned heresies,
Precepts that Cranmer's wisdom taught the prince:
The pope and we are held as heretics.
What thinkst thou, Bonner, of this wavering age?
 Bon. As seamen do of storms, yet hope for fair weather.
By'r lady, Gardiner, we must look about,
The protestants begin to gather head,
Luther has sown well, and England's ground
Is fat and fertile to increase his seed;
Here's lofty plants; what? bishops and prelates,
Ay, nobility temporal: but we shall temper all
At the return of our high cardinal.
 Gar. Bonner, 'tis true, but in mean time we must
Prevent this rancour that now swells so big,
That it must out, or break; they have a dangerous head,
And much I fear.
 Bon.   What? not the king I hope.
 Gar. 'Tis doubtful whether he will bend, but sure
Queen Katherine's a strong Lutheran; heard ye not,

How in presence of the king and cardinal
She did extirp against his holiness?
   Bon. But had our English cardinal once attain'd
The high possession of Saint Peter's chair,
He'd bar some tongues that now have scope too much;
'Tis he must do it, Gardiner, 'tis a perilous thing,
Queen Katherine can do much with England's king.
   Gar. Ay, Bonner, that's the sum of all;
There must be no queen, or the abbeys fall.
   Bon. See, where she comes with the king's sister,
And from the prince's lodging; let's salute her.

     Enter the QUEEN, LADY MARY *and Attendants.*

   Gar. Good morrow to your majesty.
   Q. Kath. Good morrow to my reverend lords of London
And Winchester; saw ye the king to-day?
   Bon. His highness was not yet abroad this morning,
But here we will attend his excellence.
   Q. Kath. Come, sister, we'll go see his majesty.
   L. Mary. We will attend ye, madam.
   Q. Kath. Set forward, gentlemen; good morrow, lords.
                                      [Exeunt Queen &c.
   Gar. Ill morrow must it be to you or us,
Conspirators 'gainst men religious.
Bonner, these Lutherans do conspire, I see,
And scoff the pope and his supremacy.
   Bon. Let's strike in time then and incense the king,
And suddenly their states to ruin bring.
The trumpets sounds, it seems the king is coming,
We'll watch and take advantage cunningly.

     Enter the KING, QUEEN, LADY MARY, BRANDON, SEYMOUR,
              GRAY, *and* DUDLEY.

   King. Where's Brandon?
   Bran. My liege.
   King. Come hither, Kate.
   Bran. Did your grace call?
   King. I'll speak wi' ye anon; I'll speak wi' ye anon!
Come, Kate, let's walk a little: who is there?
My lords of London and of Winchester, welcome, welcome!
By this your master the cardinal, I trow,
Has parted with the emperor, and set
A league between the French and him. Mother o' God!

I would ourself in person had been there,
But Wolsey's diligence we need not fear;
Ha! think ye, he will not?
    Gar. No doubt he will, my lord.
    King. Ay, Gardiner, 'twill be his best policy;
Their friendship must advance his dignity,
If e'er he get the papal governance.
    Dud. And that will never be, I hope.
    Sey. 'Twere pity it should.
    Gray. He's proud enough already.
    King. Ha! What's that ye talk there?
    Bran. They say, my lord, he's gone with such a train,
As if he should be elected presently.
    King. 'Fore God, 'tis a gallant priest! Come hither, Charles,
pr'ythee, let me lean o' thy shoulder: by Saint George, Kate,
I grow stiff, methinks.
    Q. Kath. Will't please your highness sit and rest yourself?
    King. No, no, Kate, I'll walk still; Brandon shall stay
mine arm; I'm fat and pursy and 'twill get me a stomach;
sawst the prince to-day, Kate?
    Q. Kath. Ay, my good lord.
    King. God bless him and make him fortunate.
I tell ye, lords, the hope that England hath,
Is now in him; 'fore God, I think, old Harry
Must leave ye shortly; well, God's will be done!
Here'll be old shuffling then, ha! will there not?
Well, you say nothing? I pray God there be not:
I do not like this difference in religion;
Ay, God's dear Lady, an I live
But seven years longer, we'll take order thoroughly.
    Bon. We hear that Luther out of Germany
Hath writ a book unto your majesty,
Wherein he much repents his former deeds,
Craving your highness' pardon, and withal
Submits himself unto your grace's pleasure.
    King. Bonner, 'tis true, and we have answer'd it,
Blaming at first his haughty insolence,
And now his lightness and inconstancy,
That writ, he knew not what, so childishly.
    Gar. Much bloodshed there is now in Germany
About this difference in religion,
With Lutherans, Arians, and Anabaptists,
As half the province of Helvetia

Is with their tumults almost quite destroyed.

 Q. Kath. Methinks, 'twere well, my royal sovereign,
Your grace, the emperor, and the Christian kings
Would call a council and peruse the books,
That Luther writ against the catholics,
The superstitious and the church of Rome,
And if they teach a truer way to heaven,
Agreeing with the Hebrew Testament,
Why should they not be read and followed?

 King. Thou sayst well, Kate, so they agree with the
           scriptures,
I think, 'tis lawful to peruse and read them:
Speak, bishops!

 Gar. Most unlawful, my dear sovereign,
Unless permitted by his holiness.

 Q. Kath. How prove ye that, my lord?

 King. Well said, Kate; to them again, good wench.
Lords, give us leave a while, avoid the presence,
We'll hear the bishops and my queen dispute.

 Q. Kath. I am a weak scholar, my lord,
But on condition, that your highness, nor these reverend lords
Will take no exceptions at my woman's wit,
I am content to hold the argument:
And first, with reverence to his majesty,
Tell me, why would you make the king believe,
His highness and the people under him,
Are tied so strictly to obey the pope?

 Bon. Because, fair queen, he is God's deputy.

 Q. Kath. So are all kings, and God himself commands
The king to rule and people to obey,
And both to love and honour him:
But you, that are sworn servants unto Rome,
How are ye faithful subjects to the king,
When first ye serve the pope, then after him?

 Gar. Madam, these are that sect of Lutherans,
That makes your highness so mistake the scriptures;
Your slender argument's thus answered:
Before the king God must be worshipped.

 Q. Kath. 'Tis true, but pray ye, answer this:
Suppose the king by proclamation
Commanded you and every of his subjects,
On pain of death and forfeit of his goods,
To spurn against the pope's authority:

Ye know the Scripture binds ye to obey him,
But this I think, if that his grace did so,
Your slight obedience all the world should know.
    King. God's mother, Kate, thou'st touched them there;
What say ye to that, Bonner?
    Bon. Were it to any one but her majesty,
These questions were confuted easily.
    Q. Kath. Pray, tell the king then, what Scripture have ye,
To teach religion in an unknown language?
To instruct the ignorant to kneel to Saints,
By barefoot pilgrimage to visit shrines,
For money to release from purgatory
The vildest villain, thief, or murderer?
All this the people must believe you can,
Such is the dregs of Rome's religion.
    Gar. Ay, those are the speeches of those heretics,
Of Cranmer, Ridley, and blunt Latimer,
That daily rail against his holiness,
Filling the land with hateful heresies.
    Q. Kath. Nay be not angry, nor mistake them, lords,
What they have said or done, was mildly followed,
As by their articles is evident.
    King. Where are those articles, Kate?
    Q. Kath. I'll go and fetch them to your majesty,
And pray, your highness view them graciously. [*Exit Queen.*
    King. Go, fetch them, Kate. Ah, sirrah, we have women
                      doctors!
Now I see, Mother o' God, here's a fine world the whilst,
That 'twixt so many men's opinions
The holy Scriptures must be bandied thus!
    Gar. God grant, it breed no further detriment
Unto your crown and sacred dignity:
They that would alter thus religion,
I fear they scarcely love your royal person.
    King. Ha! Take heed what you do say, Gardinor!
    Gar. My love and duty to your majesty
Bids me be bold to speak my conscience;
Unless your safety and your life they hate,
Why should they daily thus disturb the state?
To smoothe the face of false rebellion
Proud traitors will pretend religion;
For under colour of reformation,
The upstart followers of Wicklif's doctrine,

In the fifth Henry's days arose in arms,
And had not diligent care prevented them,
Their powers had suddenly surprised the king;
And, good my liege, who knows their proud intent,
That thus rebel against your government?
 King. Shrewd proofs, by'r lady and by Saint Peter!
I swear, we will not trust their gentleness.
Speak, Gardiner, and resolve us speedily,
Who's the ring-leader of this lusty crew?
 Bon. Unless your highness please to pardon us,
We dare not speak, nor urge your majesty.
 King. We pardon what ye speak, resolve us speedily.
 Gar. Then, if your royal person will be safe,
Your life preserved and this fair realm in peace,
And all these troubles smoothly pacified,
The queen, dear lord, must be removed from you.
 King. Ha! the queen? Bold sir, advise ye well,
Take heed, ye do not wrong her loyalty.
 Gar. See here, my liege, are proofs too manifest,
Her highness with a sect of Lutherans
Have private meetings, secret conventicles,
To wrest the grounds of all religion,
Seeking by tumults to subvert the state,
The which, without your majesty's consent,
Is treason capital against the crown.
 Bon. And seeing, without the knowledge of your grace,
They dare attempt these dangerous stratagems,
'Tis to be feared, which heaven, we pray, prevent,
They do conspire against your sacred life.
 Gar. Why else should all these private meetings be,
Without the knowledge of your majesty?
 King. Mother o' God, these proofs are probable,
And strong presumptions do confirm your words.
Within there, ho!

    Enter COMPTON.

 Comp. My lord.
 King. Sir William Compton, see the doors made fast,
Double our guard, let none come near our person,
Summon the council to confer with us,
Bid them attend us in the privy chamber.
 Comp. Here is a letter for your majesty
From Martin Luther out of Germany.

King. Damn'd schismatic, still will he trouble us,
With books and letters. Leave it and be gone.
[*Exit Compton.*
The villain thinks to smooth his treachery
By fawning speeches to our majesty,
But by my George, lord bishops, if I live,
I'll root his favourites from England's bounds.
What writes his worship? [*Reads the letter.*
Gar. Now, Bonner, stir, the game is set a-foot,
The king is now incensed, let's follow close,
To have queen Katherine shorter by a head;
These heresies will cease, when she is dead.
King. Holy Saint Peter, what a knave is this:
Erewhile he writ submissively to us,
And now again repents his humbleness;
Bishops, it seems, being touched with our reply,
He writes thus boldly to our majesty.
Gardiner, look here, he was deceived, he says,
'When he thought to find John Baptist in the courts of princes, or
resident with those, that are clothed in purple.'
Mother o' God, is 't not a dangerous knave?
Gar. False Luther knows, he has great friends in England,
Else durst he not thus move your majesty.
King. We'll cut his friends off, ere they grow too strong,
And sweep these vipers from our state ere long,
No marvel though queen Katherine plead for him,
That is, I see, the greatest Lutherin.
How is your counsels we proceed in these?
Bon. 'Twere best, your grace did send her to the Tower,
Before they further do confer with her.
King. Let it be so: go, get a warrant drawn,
And with a strong guard bear her to the Tower:
Our hand shall sign your large commission;
Let Cranmer from the prince be straight removed,
And come not near the court on pain of death.
Mother o' God, shall I be baffled thus
By traitors, rebels, and false heretics?
Get articles for her arraignment ready,
If she of treason be convict, I swear,
Her head goes off, were she my kingdom's heir. [*Sound. Exit.*

Enter the PRINCE, CRANMER, TYE, *and the young Lords.*

Prince. Cranmer!

Cran. My lord.
Prince. Where is Francisco, our Italian tutor?
Cran. He does attend your grace without, my lord.
Prince. Tell him, anon we will confer with him.
We'll ply our learning, Browne, least you be beaten,
We will not have your knighthood so disgraced.
Browne. I thank ye, good my lord.
An your grace would but a little ply your learning,
I warrant ye, I'll keep my knighthood from breeching.
Prince. Faith, Ned, I will.

Enter first Servant.

How now, what letter's that?
First Serv. From your grace's sister, the Lady Mary.
Prince. Come give it me, we guess at the contents.
Cranmer, my sister oft hath writ to me,
That you and bishop Bonner might confer
About these points of new religion.
Tell me, tutor, will ye dispute with him?
Cran. With all my heart, my lord, and wish the king
Would deign to hear our disputation.

Enter second Servant.

Prince. What hast thou there?
Sec. Serv. A letter from your royal sister, young Elizabeth.
Prince. Another letter ere we open this;
Well, we will view them both immediately.
I pray ye, attend us in the next chamber,
And tutors, if I call ye, not before,
Give me some notice, if the king, my father,
Be walked abroad; I must go visit him.
Tye. We will, fair prince.   [*Exeunt Cranmer and Tye.*
Prince. What says my sister Mary? She is oldest,
And by due course must first be answered.   [*Reads.*
'The blessed mother of thy redeemer with all the Angels and holy Saints be intermissers to preserve thee of idolatry, to invocate the Saints for help.'
Alas, good sister, still in this opinion!
These are thy blinded tutors, Bonner, Gardiner,
That wrong thy thoughts with foolish heresies;
I'll read no further: to him will Edward pray

For preservation that can himself preserve me,
Without the help of Saint or ceremony.
What writes Elizabeth? Sweet sister, thou'st my heart,
And of prince Edward's love hast greatest part.

> 'Sweet prince, I salute thee with a sister's love;
> Be steadfast in thy faith and let thy prayers
> Be dedicate to God only, for 'tis he alone,
> Can strengthen thee and confound thine enemies.
> Give a settled assurance of thy hopes in heaven;
> God strengthen thee in all temptations
> And give thee grace to shun idolatry,
> Heaven send thee life to inherit thy election,
> To God I commend thee, who still, I pray, preserve thee.
>   Thy loving sister ELIZABETH.'

Loving thou art and of me best beloved,
Thy lines shall be my contemplation's cures,
And in thy virtues will I meditate:
To Christ I'll only pray for me and thee;
This I embrace, away idolatry!

Enter CRANMER.

How now, Cranmer? where's the king?
   Cran. Conferring with his council, gracious prince;
There is some earnest business troubles him,
The guards are doubled and commandment given,
That none be suffer'd to come near the presence.
God keep his majesty from traitors' hands!
   Prince. Amen, good Cranmer! What should disturb him
                                  thus?
Is cardinal Wolsey yet returned from France?
   Tye. Ay, my good lord, and this day comes to court.
   Prince. Perhaps this hasty business of the king
Is touching Wolsey and his embassage.
   Cran. Pray God, it be not worse, my lord.

Enter COMPTON.

   Tye. Here comes Sir William Compton from his highness.
   Comp. Health to your excellence.
   Prince.   What news, Sir William?

  Comp. The king expects your grace's company,
And wills your highness to come and speak with him.
And, doctor Cranmer, from his majesty
I charge ye speedily to leave the court,
And come not near the prince, on pain of death,
Without direction from the king and peers.
  Cran. Sir, I obey ye; God so deal with me,
As I have wished unto his majesty.
  Prince. Cranmer banish'd the court? for what I pray?
  Comp. I know not, gracious lord; pray, pardon me,
'Tis the king's pleasure, and trust me, I am sorry,
It was my hap to bring this heavy message.
  Cran. Nay, good Sir William, your message moves not me;
My service to his royal majesty
Was always true and just, so help me heaven:
Only I pray your grace to move the king,
That I may come to trial speedily,
And if in aught I have deserved death,
Let me not draw another minute's breath. [*Exit Cranmer.*
  Comp. Will ye go, my lord?
  Prince. Not yet, we're not your prisoner, are we, sir?
  Comp. No, my dear lord.
  Prince. Then go before, and we will follow ye;
Your worship will forget yourself, I see. [*Exit Compton.*
My tutor thrust from court so suddenly?
This is strange.

     Enter TYE.

  Tye. The queen, my lord, is come to speak with you.
  Prince. Avoid the presence then and conduct her in,
I'll speak with her and after see the king.

    Enter the QUEEN.

  Q. Kath. Leave us alone, I pray ye. [*Exit Tye.*
  Prince. Your grace is welcome; how fares your majesty?
  Q. Kath. Never so ill, dear prince, for now I fear,
Even as a wretched caitiff, kill'd with care,
I am accus'd of treason, and the king
Is now in council to dispose of me:
I know his frown is death, and I shall die.
  Prince. Who are your accusers?
  Q. Kath. I know not.

Prince. How know ye then his grace is so incensed?
    Q. Kath. One of my gentlemen, passing by the presence,
Took up this bill of accusations,
Wherein twelve articles are drawn against me:
It seems my false accusers lost it there.
Here they accuse me of conspiracy,
That I with Cranmer, Latimer, and Ridley
Do seek to raise rebellion in the state,
Alter religion and bring Luther in,
And to new government inforce the king.
    Prince. Then that's the cause that Cranmer was removed;
But did your highness e'er confer with them,
As they have here accus'd ye to the king?
    Q. Kath. Never, nor ever had I one such thought,
As I have hope in him my soul hath bought.
    Prince. Then fear not, gracious madam; I'll to the king,
And doubt not but I'll make your peace with him.
    Q. Kath. O, plead for me, tell him my soul is clear,
Never did thought of treason harbour here;
As I intended to his sacred life,
So be it to my soul or joy or grief!
    Prince. Stay here till I return; I'll move his majesty,
That you may answer your accusers presently. [*Exit Prince.*
    Q. Kath. O, I shall never come to speak with him:
The lion in his rage is not so stern,
As royal Henry in his wrathful spleen,
And they that have accused me to his grace,
Will work such means, I ne'er shall see his face.
Wretched queen Katherine, would thou hadst been
Kate Parr still, and not great England's queen.

Enter COMPTON.

    Comp. Health to your majesty.
    Q. Kath. Wish me, good Compton, woe and misery;
This giddy flattering world I hate and scoff,
Ere long, I know, queen Katherine's head must off
Came ye from the king?
    Comp. I did, fair queen, and much sad tidings bring.
His grace, in secret, hath revealed to me,
What is intended to your majesty.
Which I, in love and duty to your highness,
Am come to tell ye and to counsel ye,

The best I can in this extremity.
Then on my knees I dare entreat your grace,
Not to reveal what I shall say to you,
For then I am assured that death's my due.
    Q. Kath. I will not, on my faith: good Compton, speak,
That with thy sad reports my heart may break.
    Comp. Thus then at your fair feet my life I lay,
In hope to drive your highness' cares away
You are accused of high conspiracy
And treason 'gainst his royal majesty;
So much they have incensed his excellency,
That he hath granted firm commission,
To attach your person and convey ye hence,
Close prisoner to the Tower; articles are drawn,
And time appointed for arraignment there.
Good madam, be advised by this; I know,
The officers are sent to arrest your person:
Prevent their malice, haste ye to the king,
I'll use such means that you shall speak with him;
There plead your innocence, I know his grace
Will hear ye mildly, therefore delay not:
If you be taken ere you see the king,
I fear ye never more shall speak to him.
    Q. Kath. O Compton, 'twixt thy love and my sage fear,
I feel ten thousand sad vexations here;
Lead on, I pray, I'll be advised by thee,
The king is angry, and the queen must die   *[Exeunt*

    Enter BONNER *and* GARDINER *with the commission.*

    Gar. Come, Bonner, now strike sure, the iron's hot;
Urge all thou canst, let nothing be forgot:
We have the king's hand here to warrant us,
'Twas well the cardinal came so luckily,
Who urged, the state would quite be ruined,
If that religion thus were altered,
Which made his highness, with a fiery spleen,
Direct out warrants to attach the queen.
    Bon. 'Twas excellent; that cedar once o'erthrown,
To crop the lower shrubs let us alone.
    Gar. Those articles of accusations,
We framed against her, being lost by you,
Had like to overthrow our policy,

Had we not stoutly urged his majesty.
 Bon. Well, well; what is now to be done?
 Gar. A guard must be provided speedily,
To bear her prisoner unto London Tower,
And watch convenient place to arrest her person.
 Bon. Tush! any place shall serve, for who dares contradict
His highness' hand? even from his side we'll hale her,
And bear her quickly to her longest home,
Least we and ours by her to ruin come.
 Gar. About it then, let them untimely die,
That scorn the pope and Rome's supremacy.   [*Exeunt.*

   Enter the KING *and* PRINCE, *the Guard before them.*

 King. Guard, watch the doors and let none come near us,
But such as are attendant on our person.
Mother o' God, 'tis time to stir, I see,
When traitors creep so near our majesty.
Must English Harry walk with armed guards
Now in his old age? must I fear my life
By hateful treason of my queen and wife?
 Prince. I do beseech your royal majesty,
To hear her speak ere ye condemn her thus.
 King. Go to, Ned, I charge ye speak not for her; she's
a dangerous traitor. How now, who knocks so loud there?
 First Guard. 'Tis cardinal Wolsey, my lord.
 King. An 't be the devil, tell him he comes not here:
Bid him attend us till our better leisure.
Come hither, Ned, let me confer with you;
Didst ever hear the disputation
'Twixt Cranmer and the queen about religion?
 Prince. Never, my lord: I think they never yet,
At any time, had speech concerning it.
 King. O, thou'rt deceived, Ned; it is too certain. [*Knocks.*
Heyday, more knocking? Knock irons on his heels
And bear him hence, whate'er he be disturbs us.
Who is 't?
 First Guard. Sir William Compton, good my liege.
 King. Is 't he? well, let him in.

    Enter COMPTON.

      God's holy Mother,

Here is a stir indeed; Compton, ye knock
Too loud for entrance here: you care not, though
The king be ne'er so near; say ye, sir. Ha!
    Comp. I do beseech your pardon for my boldness.
    King. Well, what's your business?
    Comp. The queen, my lord, entreats to speak with you
    King. Body o' me, is she not 'rested yet?
Why do they not convey her to the Tower?
We gave commission to attach her presently.
Where is she?
    Comp.   At the door, my sovereign.
    King. So near our presence? Keep her out, I charge ye.
Bend all your halberds' points against the door:
If she presume to enter, strike her through.
Dare she presume again to look on us?
    Prince. Upon my knees I do beseech your highness,
To hear her speak.
    King. Up, Ned, stand up! I will not look on her.
Mother o' God! stand close and guard it sure,
If she come in, I'll hang ye all, I swear.
    Prince. I do beseech your grace.
    King. Sir boy, no more; I'll hear no more of her;
Proud slut, bold traitress, and forgetful beast,
Yet dare she further move our patience.
    Prince. I'll pawn my princely word, right royal father.
She shall not speak a word to anger ye.
    King. Will you pawn your word for her? Mother o' God!
The prince of Wales his word is warrant for a king.
And we will take it, Ned; go, call her in.

Enter QUEEN.

Sir William, let the guard attend without;
Reach me a chair, all but the prince depart.
How now, what do you weep and kneel?
Does your black soul the guilt of conscience feel?
Out, out, you are a traitor.
    Q. Kath. A traitor? O you all-seeing powers,
Here witness to my lord my loyalty!
A traitor? O, then you are too merciful!
If I have treason in me, why rip you not
My ugly heart out with your weapon's point?

O, my good lord, if it hath traitorous blood,
It will be black, deform'd and tenebrous,
If not, from it will spring a scarlet fountain,
And spit defiance in their perjur'd throats,
That have accus'd me to your majesty,
Making my state thus full of misery.
    King. Canst thou deny it?
    Q. Kath. Else should I wrongfully accuse myself:
O, my dear lord, I do beseech your highness,
To satisfy your wronged queen in this:
Upon what ground grows this suspicion,
Or who thus wrongfully accuseth me
Of cursed treason 'gainst your majesty?
    King. Some probable effects myself can witness,
Others our faithful subjects testify:
Have you not oft maintained arguments,
Even to our face, against religion?
Which, join'd with other complots, show itself,
As it is gathered by our loyal subjects,
For treason capital against our person.
God's holy Mother! you'll remove us quickly
And turn me out: old Harry must away,
Now in mine age, lame, and half bed-rid,
Or else you'll keep me fast enough in prison. Ha!
Mistress, these are no hateful treasons, these?
    Q. Kath. Heaven on my forehead write my worst intent,
And let your hate against my life be bent,
If ever thought of ill against your majesty
Was harboured here, refuse me, gracious God,
To your face, my liege, if to your face I speak it;
It manifests no complot, nor no treason,
Nor are they loyal that so injure me.
What I did speak was as my woman's wit,
To hold out argument could compass it;
My puny scholarship is held too weak,
To maintain proofs about religion.
Alas, I did it but to waste the time,
Knowing as then your grace was weak and sickly,
So to expel part of your pain and grief:
And for my good intent they seek my life,
O God, how am I wronged!
    King. Ha, sayst thou so, was it no otherwise?
    Q. Kath. What should I say, that you might credit me?

If I am false, heaven strike me suddenly!

King. Body o' me! what everlasting knaves
Are these that wrong thee thus! Alas, poor Kate!
Come, stand up, stand up! Wipe thine eyes, wipe thine
eyes! 'Fore God, 'twas told me thou wert a traitor: I could
hardly think it, but that it was applied so hard to me. God's
Mother, Kate, I fear my life, I tell ye; King Harry would
be loth to die by treason now, that has bid so many brunts
unblemished, yet I confess, that now I grow stiff: my legs
fail me first, but they stand furthest from my heart and that's
still sound, I thank my God. Give me thy hand, come kiss
me, Kate: so, now I'm friends again. Whoreson knaves,
crafty varlets, make thee a traitor to old Harry's life! Well,
well, I'll meet with some of them! 'S foot! Come, sit on my
knee, Kate!
Mother o' God! he that says thou'rt false to me,
By England's crown, I'll hang him presently.

Q. Kath. When I have thought of ill against your state,
Let me be made the vildest reprobate.

King. That's my good Kate, but by th' Mary God,
Queen Katherine, you must thank prince Edward here,
For but for him thou'dst gone to th' Tower, I swear.

Q. Kath. I shall be ever thankful to his highness,
And pray for him and for your majesty.

King. Come, Kate, we'll walk awhile i' th' garden here:
Who keeps the door there?

Comp. My lord.

King. Sir William Compton, take my ring,
Bid doctor Cranmer haste to court again;
Give him that token of king Henry's love,
Discharge our guards, we fear no traitor's hand,
Our state, beloved of all, doth firmly stand:
Go, Compton.

Comp. I go, my lord.

King. Bid Wolsey haste him to our royal presence;
Great Charles, the mighty Roman Emperor,
Our nephew and the hope of Christendom,
Is come to see his uncle and the English court;
We'll entertain him with imperial port. [*Exit Compton.*
Come hither, Ned.

Enter BONNER *and* GARDINER *with the Guard.*

Gar. Fellows, stay there, and when I call, come forward;

The service you pursue is for the king,
Therefore I charge ye to perform it boldly:
We have his hand and seal to warrant it.
 First Guard. We'll follow you with resolution, sir;
The church is on our side, what should we fear?
 Gar. See, yonder she is talking with his majesty;
Think you, we may attempt to take her here?
 Bon. Why should we not? have we not firm commission,
To attach her anywhere? Be bold and fear not;
Fellows, come forward.
 King.   How now, what's here to do?
 Q. Kath. The bishops, it seems, my lord, would speak
       with you.
 King. With bills and halberds? Well, tarry there, Kate.
I'll go myself. Now, wherefore come you?
 Gar. As loyal subjects to your state and person,
We come to apprehend that traitorous woman.
 King. Ye are a couple of drunken knaves and varlets!
God's holy Mother! she's more true and just
Than any prelate that suborns the pope,
Thus to usurp upon our government.
Call you her traitor? Ye are lying beasts
And false conspirators.
 Bon. Your majesty hath seen what proofs we had.
 King. Hear you, Bonner, you are a whoreson coxcomb;
What proofs had ye, but treasons of your own inventions?
 Q. Kath. O dear my lord, respect the reverend bishops,
Bonner and Gardiner loves your majesty.
 King. Alas, poor Kate, thou thinkst full little what they
      come for:
Thou hast small reason to commend their loves,
That falsely have accused thy harmless life.
 Q. Kath. O God, are these mine enemies?
 Gar. We have your highness' hand to warrant it.
 King. Let's see it then.
 Gar. 'Tis here, my liege.
 King. So, now ye've both my hands to contradict
What one hand did: and now our word again
Shall serve as warrant to bear you both
As prisoners to the Fleet,
Where you shall answer this conspiracy.
You, fellows, that came to attach the queen,
Lay hands on them and bear them to the Fleet.

Q. Kath. O, I beseech your highness on my knees,
Remit the doom of their imprisonment.
King. Stand up, good Kate, thou wroug'st thy majesty,
To plead for them that thus have injured thee.
Q. Kath. I have forgot it and do still entreat
Their humble pardons at your gracious feet.
King. Mother o' God, what a foolish woman's this!
Well, for her sake we will revoke our doom,
But come not near us, as you love your lives:
Away and leave us, you are knaves and miscreants,
Whoreson caitiffs—come to attach my queen!
Q. Kath. Vex not, my lord, it will distemper you.
King. Mother o' God, I'll temper some on them for't.

Enter BRANDON.

How now, Brandon?
  Bran. The emperor, my lord.
  King. Get a train ready there: Charles Brandon, come
We'll meet the monarch of imperial Rome.
Go, Ned, prepare yourself to meet the emperor,
We'll send you further notice of our pleasure.

Enter CARDINAL *and* WILL.

Attend the prince there. Welcome, lord cardinal!
Hath not your tedious journey into France
Disturb'd your grace's health and reverend person?
  Will. No, no, ne'er fear him, Harry, he has got more by the journey; he'll be pope shortly.
  King. What, William! how chance I have not seen you to-day? I thought you would not have been the hindmost man to salute me.
  Will. No more I am not, Harry, for yonder is Patch behind me, I could never get him before me, since thou conjuredst him i' th' great chamber; all the horses i' th' town cannot haul him into thy presence, I warrant thee.
  King. Will he not come in?
  Will. Not for the world, he stands watching at the door, he'll not stir while the cardinal come; then the fool will follow him everywhere.
  Wol. I thank you, William, I am beholding to you still.
  Will. Nay, my lord, I am more beholding unto you, I

thank your fool for it: we have ransacked your wine-cellars since you went into France. Do you blush, my lord? Nay, that's nothing, you have wine there is able to set a colour in any man's face, I warrant it.

King. Why, William, is the cardinal's wine so good?

Will. Better than thine, I'll be sworn; I'll take but two handfuls of his wine and it shall fill four hogsheads of thine —look here else!

Wol. Mordieu!

Will. More Devil! is't not? for without conjuring you could never do it. But I pray you, my lord, call upon *Mordieu* no longer, but speak plain English: you have deceived the king in French and Latin long enough, o' conscience.

King. Is his wine turned into gold, Will?

Wol. The fool mistakes, my gracious sovereign.

Will. Ay, ay, my lord, ne'er set your wit to the fool's: Will Summers will be secret now and say nothing; if I would be a blab of my tongue, I could tell the king how many barrels full of gold and silver there was: six tuns filled with plate and jewels, twenty great trunks with crosses, crosiers, copes, mitres, maces, golden crucifixes, besides the four hundred and twelve thousand pound that the poor chimneys paid for Peter pence. But this is nothing, for when you are pope, you may pardon yourself for more knaveries than this comes to.

King. Go to, fool, you wrong the cardinal;
But grieve not, Wolsey: William will be bold.
I pray you, set on to meet the emperor,
The mayor and citizens are gone before,
The prince of Wales shall follow presently,
And with our George and collar of estate,
Present him with the order of the Garter.
Great Maximilian, his progenitor,
Upon his breast did wear the English cross,
And underneath our standard marched in arms,
Receiving pay for all his warlike host;
And Charles with knighthood shall be honoured.
Begin, lord cardinal, greet his majesty,
And we ourself will follow presently.

Wol. I go, my sovereign.

Will. Fair weather after ye: well, an e'er he come to be pope, I shall be plunged for this.

Q. Kath. William, you have anger'd the cardinal, I can tell you.

King. 'Tis no matter, Kate, I'll anger him worse ere long,
Though for awhile I smooth it to his face:
I did suspect what here the fool hath found.
He keeps forsooth a High Court Legatine,
Taxing our subjects, gathering sums of gold,
Which he belike hath hid to make him pope.
A' God's name let him, that shall be our own.
But to our business; come, queen Katherine,
You shall with us to meet the emperor:
Let all your ladies be in readiness.
Go, let our guard attend the prince of Wales:
Upon ourself the Lords and Pensioners
Shall give attendance in their best array; [*Sound.*
Let all estates be ready: come, fair Kate,
The emperor shall see our English state. [*Sound. Exeunt.*

Enter EMPEROR, CARDINAL, MAYOR, *and Gentlemen.*

Wol. Your majesty is welcome into England,
The king, our master, will rejoice to see
Great Charles', the royal emperor's, majesty.

Emp. We thank your pains, my good lord cardinal,
And much our longing eyes desire to see
Our kingly uncle and his princely son,
And therefore, when you please, I pray, set on.

Wol. On, gentlemen, and meet the prince of Wales,
That comes fore-runner to his royal father,
To entertain the Christian emperor.
Meanwhile your majesty may here behold
This warlike kingdom's fair metropolis,
The City London and the river Thames,
And note the situation of the place.

Emp. We do, my lord, and count it admirable:
But see, lord cardinal, the prince is coming.

Enter the PRINCE *with a Herald before him, bearing the Collar and Garter, the Guard and Lords attending.*

Emp. Well met, young cousin.
Prince.   I kiss your highness' hand,
And bid you welcome to my father's land:
I shall not need infer comparisons.

Welcome beyond compare, for so your excellency
Hath honour'd England, in containing you,
As with all princely pomp and state we can,
We'll entertain great Charles, the Austrian.
And first, in sign of honour to your grace,
I here present this collar of estate,
This golden garter of the knighthood's order,
An honour to renown the emperor.
Thus, as my father has commanded me,
I entertain your royal majesty.

Emp. True-honoured offspring of a famous king,
Thou dost amaze me and dost make me wish,
I were a second son to England's lord,
In interchange of my imperial seat,
To live with thee, fair hope of majesty;
So well our welcome we accept of thee,
And with such princely spirit pronounce the word,
Thy father's state can no more state afford.

Prince. Yes, my good lord, in him there's majesty,
In me there's love with tender infancy.   [*Sound trumpets.*
Wol. The trumpets sound, my lord, the king is coming.
Prince. Go all of you, attend his royal person,
Whilst we observe the emperor's majesty.   [*Sound.*

Enter the Heralds first, then the Trumpets, next the Guard, then Mace Bearer and Swords, then the CARDINAL, *then* BRANDON, *then the* KING, *after him the* QUEEN, LADY MARY, *and Ladies attending.*

King. Hold! stand, I say.
Bran.   Stand gentlemen.
Wol. Cease those trumpets there.
King. Is the emperor yet come in sight of us?
Wol. His majesty is hard at hand, my lord.
King. Then, Brandon, sheathe our sword and bear our
                            maces down,
In honour of my lord the emperor.
Forward again!

Bran. On, gentlemen, afore, sound trumpets and set forward.
Prince. Behold my father, gracious emperor.
Emp. We'll meet him, cousin.
Uncle of England, king of France and Ireland,
Defender of the ancient Christian Faith,

With greater joy I do embrace thy breast,
Than when the seven electors crowned me,
Great emperor of the Christian monarchy.
    King. Great Charles, the first Emperor of Almain, King
of the Romans, Semper Augustus, warlike King of Spain and
Sicily, both Naples, Navarre and Aragon, King of Crete and
great Jerusalem, Archduke of Austria, Duke of Milan, Brabant,
Burgundy, Tyrol, and Flanders,
With this great title I embrace thy breast,
And how thy sight doth please, suppose the rest.
Sound trumpets, while my fair queen Katherine
Gives entertainment to the emperor.   [*Sound.*
Welcome again to England, princely cousin!
We dwell here but in an outward continent,
Where winter's icicles hangs on our beards,
Bord'ring upon the frozen Orcades,
Our mother-point, compass'd with th' Arctic Sea,
Where raging Boreas flies from winter's mouth;
Yet are our bloods as hot, as where the sun doth rise;
We have no golden mines to lead you to,
But hearts of proof, and what we speak we'll do.
    Emp. We thank you, uncle, and now must chide you:
If we be welcome to your country,
Why is the ancient league now broke betwixt us?
Why have your heralds in the French king's cause
Breathed defiance 'gainst our dignity,
When face to face we met at Landersey?
    King. My heralds to defy your majesty?
Your grace mistakes, we sent ambassadors
To treat a peace between the French and you,
Not to defy you as an enemy.
    Emp. Yet, uncle, in King Henry's name he came,
And boldly to our face did give the same.
    Wol. Hell stop that fatal-boding emperor's throat,
That sings 'gainst us this dismal raven's note.
    King. Mother o' God, if this be true, we see,
There are more kings in England now than we.
Where's cardinal Wolsey? Heard you this news in France?
    Wol. I did, my liege, and by my means 'twas done:
I'll not deny 't, I had commission,
To join a league betwixt the French and him,
Which he withstanding as an enemy,
I did defy him from your majesty.

King. Durst thou presume so, base-born cardinal,
Without our knowledge to abuse our name?
Presumptuous traitor, under what pretence
Didst thou attempt to brave the emperor?
Belike thou meanst to level at a crown,
But thy ambitious crown shall hurl thee down.
  Wol. With reverence to your majesty, I did no more,
Than I can answer to the holy see.
  King. Villain, thou canst not answer it to me,
Nor shadow thy insulting treachery.
How durst ye, sirrah, in your embassage,
Unknown to us, stamp in our royal coin
The base impression of your cardinal's hat,
As if you were co-partner in the crown?
Ego et Rex meus: you and your king must be
In equal state, and pomp, and majesty:
Out of my presence, hateful impudence!
  Wol. Remember, my liege, that I am cardinal,
And deputy unto his holiness.
  King. Be the devil's deputy, I care not, I,
I'll not be baffled by your treachery;
You're false abusers of religion,
You can corrupt it and forbid the king,
Upon the penalty of the pope's black curse,
If he should pawn his crown for soldiers' pay,
Not to suppress an old religious abbey,
Yet you at pleasure have subverted four,
Seizing their lands, tunning up heaps of gold,
Secret conveyance of our royal seal,
To raise collections to enrich thy state,
For which, sir, we command you leave the court:
We here discharge you of your offices,
You that are Caiphas, or great cardinal,
Haste ye with speed unto your bishopric,
There keep you, until you hear further from us.
Away and speak not.
  Wol. Yet will I proudly pass as cardinal,
Although this day define my heavy fall.
  Emp. I fear, king Henry, and my royal uncle,
The cardinal will curse my progress hither.
  King. No matter, cousin; beshrew his treacherous heart,
He's moved my blood to much impatience.
Where is Will Summers?

Enter WILL SUMMERS.

Come on, wise William,
For we must use your little wits, to chase
This anger from our blood again: what art thou doing?

Will. I am looking round about the emperor, methinks 'tis a strange sight, for though he have seen more fools than I, yet I never saw more emperors but him.

Emp. Is this Will Summers? I have heard of him in all the princes' courts in Christendom.

Will. La ye, my lord, you have a famous fool of me, I can tell ye,
Will Summers is known far and near, ye see.

King. Ay, are you rhyming, William? nay, then I am for ye, I have not rhymed with ye a great while, and now I'll challenge ye, and the emperor shall be judge between us.

Will. Content, my lord, I am for ye all: come but one at once, and I care not.

King. Say ye so, sir? Come, Kate, stand by me: We'll put him to a non-plus presently.

Q. Kath. To him, Will.

Will. I warrant you, madam.

King. Answer this, sir:
        The bud is spread,
        The rose is red,
        The leaf is green.

Will.   A wench, 'tis said,
        Was found in your bed,
        Besides the queen.

Q. Kath. God a mercy for that, Will: there's two angels for thee; i'faith, my lord, I am glad I know it.

King. God's Mother, Kate, wilt thou believe the fool? He lies, he lies; ah, sirrah William, I perceive, an't had been so, you would have shamed me before the emperor: yet, William, have at you once more.
        In yonder tower,
        There is a flower,
        That hath my heart.

Will.   Within this hour,
        She pissed full sour,
        And let a fart.

Emp. He's too hard for you, my lord; I'll try him one venue myself. What say you to this, William?

             An emperor is great,
             High is his seat,
             Who is his foe?
Will.   The worms that shall eat
             His carcass for meat,
             Whether he will or no.
Emp. Well answered, Will; yet once more I am for ye.
             A ruddy lip,
             With a cherry tip,
             Is fit for a king.
Will.   Ay, so he may dip
             About her hip
             In the t'other thing.
Emp. He's put me down, my lord.
Will. Who comes next then?
King. The queen, William; look to yourself. To him, Kate!
Q. Kath. Come on, William, answer to this: —
             When cold I take,
             My head doth ache,
             What physic's good?
Will.   Here's one will make
             The cold to break,
             And warm your blood.
Q. Kath. I am not repulsed at first, William: again, sir.
             Women and their wills
             Are dangerous ills,
             As some men suppose.
Will.   She that puddings fills,
             When snow lies o' th' hills,
             Must keep clean her nose.
King. Enough, good William, you're too hard for all. —
My lord the emperor, we delay too long
Your promised welcome to the English court.
The honourable order of the Garter
Your majesty shall take immediately,
And sit install'd therewith in Windsor Castle:
I tell ye, there are lads girt with that order,
That will ungird the proudest champion. —
Set forward there, regard the emperor's state!
First in our court we'll banquet merrily,
Then mount on steeds, and girt in complete steel,

We'll tug at barriers, tilt, and tournament.
Then shall ye see the yeomen of my guard
Wrestle, shoot, throw the sledge, or pitch the bar,
Or any other active exercise.
These triumphs past, we'll forthwith haste to Windsor,
Saint George's knight shall be the Christian Emperor.
[*Exeunt omnes.*

NOTES.

P. 3.

And lord Bonnivet] Both Qs writ this name *Bonnevet*.

To move Campeius] Both Qs throughout *Campeus*. Hall, Holinshed, and the first Folio of Shakespeare, however, write *Campeius*.

If Wolsey be made pope of Rome] Should this line be intended to rhyme with the following—which I think not unlikely—it would be another proof of the varying pronunciation of the word 'Rome'. The case is strengthened by the rhyme—if rhyme it be—'come' and 'Rome' on p. 18 and p. 71. Observe also the rhyme 'home' and 'come' on p. 66. On the other hand on p. 58 QD reads: *Such is the dregs of Roome's religion*. Compare Dyce's Glossary s. Rome.

Enter Bonner] In the Qs this stage-direction follows the words: *How now, Bonner*.

P. 4.

Wol. Delay him awhile &c.] When does Bonner make his exit? If after these words of the cardinal, to execute his order, who is then to call Sir William Compton in (at p. 4)? Would it, on the other hand, become him to witness the conversation between the cardinal and the ambassadors?

I have, and by the king's means] The article is omitted in QB.

P. 5.

To invocate for her sound prosperous help] Thus QB. QD: *To invocate her sound and prosperous help*.

And all may honour thee] QB: *my honour thee*.

As Hannibal with oil did melt the Alps] The author's memory seems to have failed him, for both Appian and Livy, from either of whom he has taken this allusion, do not mention oil, but acid. Livy's words (b. XXI, ch. 37) are these: 'Inde ad rupem muniendam, per quam unam via esse poterat, milites ducti, cum cædendum esset saxum, arboribus circa immanibus deiectis detruncatisque struem ingentem lignorum faciunt, eamque (cum et vis venti apta faciendo igni coorta esset) succendunt ardentiaque saxa infuso aceto putrefaciunt. Ita torridam incendio rupem ferro pandunt, molliunt'—Appian. Hannibal ch. 4 p. 536. Compare Polybius b. III, ch. 54 and 55, whose narrative, however, is somewhat different. English translations of Appian and Livy were published in 1578 and 1600 respectively. Possibly one of them may have introduced the oil instead of the acid, which of course would decide the point.

And match'd their aged king] QB: *and march.*

P. 6.

As we directed, to the shrieves of London] QB and QD: *to the Sheriffes of London.* Three lines below both Qs read: *and the Sherive attends for them.*

For ordering those brothels &c.] See Holinshed (1586, p. 972): 'In the latter end of March (1546) the brothell houses called the Stues on the banke side in Southworke were conuerted from such filthie uses by the king's commandement, the bawds and ruffians being put out, and other persons of honest behavior placed in their rooms to inhabit in the same houses. This was done by proclamation and sound of trumpet by an herald of armes.'

Bon. They are ready, my lord, &c.] We should read: *They're ready, and the shrieve attends for them.*

Thou wilt never be able &c.] I think we should read: *Thou'lt ne'er be able half this time to sit.*

She'll wake you ere 't be long] QD: *wake you eer long.*

Exceed not her expect] Compare Dyce, Shakespeare's Works, 2d Ed., VI, 18. 104, n. 19.

She'll hear his embassage] Both Qs: *She will hear this embassage.*

That m^{a}ke all nations &c.] Qy: *that makes all nations &c.?*

P. 7.

But sight of thee, unequalled potentate] Both Qs: *unequall potentate.*

Thou art now a right woman &c.] The lame epithet '*goodly*' spoils the metre. The verse should be read: *Thou'rt now a right woman, chief of thy sex.*

Did thefi define the name of woman] Both Qs: *the name of women.*

Come, love, thou art sad, &c.] Qy: *Come, love, thou'rt sad: go, call Will Summers in?* QB reads: *call Will Summers in, to,* and begins the following line with: *Make.*

John de Mazo] My endeavours to verify this name have been in vain. In Lord Cherbury's Life and Reign of K. Henry VIII. (ed. 1649 p. 75) this bishop of Paris is called Estienne de Poncher. According to the same authority the train of the two ambassadors amounted to 1200 people.

King. Let their welcome &c.] Perhaps: *Now let their welcome*, or: *Well, let their welcome &c.*

King. Spare for no cost, &c.] Both Qs read: *Spare for no cost, Compton, what newes?*

Comp. Th' ambassadors &c.] The article is omitted in both Qs.

Give them entertainment &c.] Both Qs: *give them entertainment, Lord | Charles Brandon.*

Go and conduct them] Both Qs: *go conduct them.*

Enter Will Summers &c.] The contents of this conversation between the king and his fool are repeated in Samuel Rowland's 'Good and Bad Newes' (1622) in the following words:
'Will Sommers once unto King Harry came,
And in a serious shew himself did frame
To goe to London, taking of his leaue.
Stay, William (quoth the king) I doe perceiue
You are in haste; but tell me your occasion:
Let me prevail thus by a friends perswasion.—
Quoth he, if thou wilt know, Ile tell thee marry:
I goe to London for Court-newes, old Harry.—
Goest thither from the Court to hear Court-newes?
This is a tricke, Sommers, that makes me muse.
Oh, yes (quoth William) citizens can show
Whats done in Court ere thou and I doe know'
If an Embassador be comming over,
Before he doe arrive and land at Dover
They know his master's message and intent,
Ere thou canst tell the cause why he is sent.
If of a Parliament they doe but heare,
They know what lawes shall be enacted there.
And, therefore, for a while, adue Whitehall.
Harry, Ile bring thee newes home, lyes and all.'
Thus far the passage is quoted in Mr. Collier's 'Fools and Jesters with a Reprint of Robert Armin's Nest of Ninnies', printed for the Shakespeare Society, p. 63 seq.

P. 8.

A conduit-head keeper] QB: *a cund-head keeper.* QD: *a cundid-headkeeper.* Compare Beaumont and Fletcher, The Knight of the Burning Pestle IV, 5: *Cit*[*izen*]: Let Ralph come out on May-day in the morning, and speak upon a conduit, with all his scarfs about him, and his feathers, and his rings, and his knacks.— —*Ralph:* For from the top of Conduit-Head, as plainly may appear, I will both tell my name to you, and wherefore I came here.

One of the old women waterbearers] Both Qs: *Waterbeares.* Compare Nash, Summer's Last Will and Testament (A Select Collection of Old Plays, 1825, IX, 71): 'These waterbearers will empty the conduit and a man's coffers at once.'

Then you heard of the ambassadors] Both Qs: *Then you heare.*

They say the reason is] QB: *the reason on is.*

And now it is thought] QB: *and how it is thought.*

The women at a bake-house] QB: *at a back-house.*

The great bell in Glastonbury c.] Both Qs: *the great bell in Glassenberie: For has told twice.*

P. 9.

Crying Saint George for England] According to Mr. Collier (A Select Collection of Old Plays, 1825, IX, 49) 'this was the common cry of the English soldiers in attacking an enemy.'

God's me, thou hast] Both Qs: *th' hast.*

I may leave the presence] QB: *thy presence.*

Make wholesome fires] Perhaps an allusion to some ingredients in the fire, which superstition may have considered wholesome in a childbed-room.

Now Jane, God! bring me &c.] Both Qs give this line without any punctuation.

And help you in your weakest passions] This verse should be given to Compton instead of Dudley, to whose part only the two following lines should belong.

Long and happy reign] QD: *long and prosperous reign.*

I fear I never shall behold] Both Qs: *I shall never behold.*

Make haste and dispatch this] QB omits '*and*'.

P. 10.

Most fair commends] QD: *commend.*

Held 'twixt the realms] Both Qs: *Held betwixt.*

Our answer shall be swift] QD: *wall be swift.*

These lords shall be your guests] Both Qs: *these shall be your guests.*

Exeunt Wolsey and Ambassadors] Both Qs give only: *Ex. Woolsie*, and place this stage-direction before the verse which contains the order of the king to withdraw.

Now, Will, are you not deceiv'd] Thus both Qs. Perhaps we should read: *Now, Will, an't you deceived &c.*

P. 11.

As much purpose as the other] QD: *others.*

Such an old Dies Veneris] Qy: *Lues Veneris?*

To get her with prince] Both Qs: *he get her &c.*

Call for more woman's help] Both Qs: *more women's help.*

Do you hear. Madam Mary &c.] In both Qs these verses are printed as prose.

P. 12.

And be it son or daughter] QB omits '*or*'.

All woman's help is past] QD: *all women's help.* The sense is not: the help of all women is past, but: all the help that woman can afford, is past.

Or if it life receive] QB: *receives.*

That is my sum of bliss] QB: *that is some of blisse.*

May more children give] '*More*' is to be pronounced as a dissyllable. See Mr. Abbott's Shakespearian Grammar 480.

Exeunt ladies] QB: *Exit ladies.* QD: *Exit Lad.* In both Qs this stage-direction is added to the next line but one.

P. 13.

(That sees all in his creation)] Both Qs: *(that sees all) in his creation.*

Some impotent and coward spirit] QB: *cowardly.*

Least he should blur our fame] Both Qs regularly write '*least*' for '*lest*'.

(The fifth Henry)] QB: *(the first Henrie)*. QD: *(the Henrie)*.

Comp. My Lord?] Both Qs omit the prefix: *Comp.*

Exit Compton] This and the following stage-direction (*Enter Lady Mary &c.*) have been added by me.

But with the sad report] The article is omitted in QB.

Least both do perish] QB: *doth perish.*

So precious to our soul] QD: *to our life.*

Which with my conquering sword] Both Qs: *with me conquering sword.*

Exeunt ladies] This stage-direction is not in the Qs.

P. 14.

Joy be it, good lord Seymour] Both Qs: *Joy, be it good, lord Seymour.*

Sey. Get comfort] Both Qs: *Yet comfort.*

'Tis woman's woe] Both Qs: *this woman's woe.*

Enter Countess of Salisbury &c.] Both Qs: *Enter two Ladies.* The abbreviation '*Count.*', however, which is prefixed to the following speech, leaves no doubt as to who is meant.

See here your flesh and bone] QD: *and your bone.*

Look, royal lord] Both Qs: *Looke heere, Royall Lord.*

King. Ha, little cakebread] Both Qs give this verse to lord Seymour.

Enter Lady Mary &c.] Both Qs: *Enter Mary, and one Lady.*

Nay, then my heart misgives] Perhaps this line was intended to rhyme with the preceding and we should read: *then does my heart misgive.*

Thy silent eye] Both Qs contain this blunder; there can be no doubt, that the true reading is: *Thy silent tongue.*

Of thy troubled spirit] QD: *of my troubled spirit.*

That cannot help myself] QB: *thyself.*

P. 15.

She's left part of herself] Both Qs: *She hath left.*

To the land a prince] Both Qs: *unto the land.*

NOTES.   89

Phœnix Jana obiit &c.] Both Qs read: *obit* and add '*dolendum*' to the pentameter instead of the hexameter. — Holinshed, from whom this distich is taken, has '*incet*' for '*obiit*'.

Saint Edward's even, my lord] The metre seems to require either '*e'en*' or '*eve*'. — 'In October, says Holinshed (1586) p. 944, on Saint Edward's even (1537), which falleth on the twelfth of that month, at Hampton Court the queen was delivered of her son named Edward, for whose birth great joy was made thorough the realm. — — But as joy is often mixed with sorrow so at that time it came to pass by the death of his mother, that noble and virtuous lady queen Jane, which departed out of this life the fourteenth day of this month of October, to the great grief of the whole realm: but namely the king her husband took it most grievously of all other, who removing to Westminster there kept himself close a great while after.' — The date of the queen's death as given by Hall and Holinshed is wrong, as she did not die before the 24. of October.

Edward shall be his name!] Thus both Qs. Qy: *Edward be his name?* — The stage-direction '*Exeunt*' has been added.

Bonner and Gardiner] QB writes '*Gardner*', QD: '*Gardiner*'.

Therefore I pray you] Both Qs omit '*you*', to the detriment of the metre.

Shall be forthwith sent] Tis is the reading of both Qs. The same unusual accentuation occurs again on p. 79: —
These triumphs past we'll forthwith haste to Windsor.

And for the business] In QB the article is omitted.

Wol. Happily speed] Qy: *Speed happily?*

And pray your king remember] I am answerable for the addition of '*and*', as also for the stage-direction '*Exeunt*' five lines below.

Will cause new trouble] QB: *troubles*.

P. 16.

Re-enter Bonner] This stage-direction is not in the Qs.

Ever since the death] Probably: *For ever since the death*.

P. 17.

Hey day, tirri &c.] Both Qs: *hey, da, tere, dedell, dey, day*.

Enter King within] That is to say, on the wellknown balcony, in the background of the stage, which here represents the gallery, where, according to Sir William Compton, the king is walking.

And if you find his grace] This is the reading of both Qs; '*and*' should be struck out.

And stout Pearsie &c.] Whether the person meant be a Percy, I am unable to decide, no such person being mentioned in either Hall or Holinshed. The metre of the line is no less doubtful, unless '*stout*' be taken for a dissyllable. Or should we read: *And stout Earl Percy?* In the following verse both Qs add '*late*' before the words '*put to death.*'

Than ever was &c.] Thus both Qs.

P. 18.

And all his fair posterity] '*All*' is not in the Qs.

Exit] This stage-direction has been added.

How chance] See Shakespearian Grammar 37. Compare p. 71: *How chance I have not seen you?*

Seeing him chafe so at Charles here] These words would seem to refer to the cardinal's fool, Patch, for they cannot refer to Charles Brandon, the speech being addressed to him.

I fell over five barrels] '*I*' is not in the Qs.

Into the bottom of the cellar] QD: *in the bottom*.

And I'll venture] QB: *and ile enter*. QD: *venter*.

P. 19.

Thou fawning beast] The metre requires the addition of the pronoun '*thou*', though it is in neither of the Qs.

Where's Brandon, Surrey &c.] Instead of '*Surrey*' we ought to read '*Dudley*', there being no Surrey among the characters of the play.

Where is your council now?] An evident mistake for '*our council*'.

Enter Pages] This stage-direction is taken from QD.

Here's stuff at th' other side] These words evidently refer to the garter, which the first page is tying round the king's leg.

Be bandied thus?] Both Qs: *bebanded thus*.

To the Page] This stage-direction is an editorial addition again.

The Burkes rebel &c.] Either 'Ireland' is to be pronounced as a trisyllable, or we should read: *do the Burkes rebel.*

And with their stubborn kerns &c.] Both Qs: *his stubborn kerns*. — Roads for *inroads*; compare K. Henry V, 1, 2: *Against the Scot, who will make road upon us*; Coriolanus III, 1: *Ready, when time shall prompt them, to make road Upon's again.*

P. 20.

I'll make thee amends for it] Thus both Qs. We should either read: *I'll make amends for it*, or: *I'll make thee 'mends for it.*

That we have ill May-days] 'Ill May-day' is the name of that 'burliburly', as Holinshed terms it, which took place at London on May 1, 1518, and was chiefly directed against the numerous aliens and strangers, who took 'the living from all the artificers and the intercourse from all merchants, whereby poverty is so much increased.' John Lincoln, the author of Ill May-day, was executed in Cheapside; on the rest, 400 men and 11 women, the king himself sat in judgment in Westminster Hall (May 22) and pardoned them.

Exeunt Wolsey, lords, &c.] Both this and the following stage-direction have been added.

And nobody dare speak to him] See Mr. Abbott's Shakespearian Grammar 361.

An he go a-boxing] QB: *go boxing.*

P. 21.

Give me it, cousin] Compare p. 41: *Give me it again &c.*

As thou wert a foot-ball] QB: *an thou wert &c.*

Who's that stands laughing there?] QD: *that which stands laughing there.*

P. 22.

Will. I'd know, whether &c.] Both Qs: *He know &c.*

He sent this silly ass] The personal pronoun is not in the Qs.

Will. Because I'd have him &c.] Both Qs: *ile have him.* QD: *my fury*, instead of: *thy fury.*

I knew, how the matter stood] Both Qs: *I know &c.*

The lords has attended here] Thus both Qs.

To chop off their heads for it] QD omits: *heads*.

Continuedst in] Both Qs: *continuest in*.

If thou keptst it] QB: *keepst*.

But I'd make thee] QB: *but ile make thee*.

And cap for this] QB: *and a cap*.

King. He shall keep his word, Will; &c.] Perhaps: *Will* (or: *Well?*), *he shall keep his word; &c.* which would make a regular verse.

Enter Brandon and other lords] This stage-direction is not in the Qs.

P. 23.

He'd fain be gone] Both Qs: *Heele fain*.

He smells terribly] QD: *smelleth*.

Exeunt] An editorial addition.

Enter Campeius &c.] Both Qs: *Enter Lords and Legates*.

Sey. Gentlemen, dispatch &c.] Qy: *Go, gentlemen, dispatch &c?*

P. 24.

Of this dignity] Both Qs: *of his dignity*.

Go, Gray, and see it done] '*And*' has been added.

Trumpets, follow me] Qy: *come, trumpets, follow me?*

Would send an army to assail the Turk &c.] According to Holinshed this demand of the pope was put to the king four years before he received the title, which latter, moreover, was not sent through Cardinal Campeius, but in a bull (February 1523). 'But for the chiefest errand, says Holinshed, that this cardinal Campeius came (in 1519), he could have no toward answer: which was (as you have heard) to have levied a sum of money by way of tenths in this realm, to the maintenance of the war in defence of the Christian confines against the Turk.'

Will. Ay when? Can ye tell?] Both Qs: *I, when can ye tell?*

P. 25.

The true faith is able to defend itself &c.] In a forgotten work entitled 'Heinrich VIII. König von England und seine

Familie. Ein historisches Gemälde von C. D. Voss (Leipzig, 1792, 2 vols.)' I find the following passage (vol. I, p. 81): 'Allein sein (viz. the king's) Hofnarr Patsch, dem seine Narrheit das Recht gab, kluge Wahrheiten zu sagen, meinte: dieser Titel sei doch auch wol nicht viel mehr werth als seine Schellenkappe. "Ich bitte dich, lieber Heinrich, sagte er, lass uns nur uns selbst vertheidigen, der Glaube wird sich wohl auch schon ohne dich zu beschützen wissen."' It is greatly to be regretted that the author has not given the source of this anecdote.

Good faith! 'tis not worth] Both Qs: *as for the Popes faith (good faiths) not worth &c.*

Cam. We take our leave] The stage-direction '*Exit*' should not be added to this line, but to the next.

King. 'Tis well. Brandon &c.] Both Qs: '*Tis well, but Brandon &c.* — to the detriment of the metre.

P. 26.

Baynard's Castle] See Dyce's Glossary and Nares.

Exeunt] Both Qs: *Exit*.

Prichall, the cobbler] '*Prichall*' seems to be meant for '*Prickawl*'.

Const. Come, neighbours;] In order to restore the metre, '*come*' should be repeated after '*neighbours*'.

Was committed lately] QD: *late*.

There are two strangers &c.] Both Hall (ed. London, 1809, p. 815) and Holinshed relate the murder of these two strangers in the following words: 'In this year (1534) it chanced thas two merchant strangers fell in love with a harlot, which wat called Wolfe's wife, and this harlot had often haunted the strangers' chambers. And so on a time the said harlot appointed these strangers to come to Westminster and she had prepared for them a boat, in which boat was but one man to row which was a strong thief, and in the end of the boat lay Wolfe, her husband, covered with a leather that boatmen use to cover their cushions with, and so these strangers sat them down mistrusting nothing. Now when this boatman had brought them as far as a place called the Turning Tree, suddenly stepped up the said Wolfe, and with his dagger thrust the one of them through: the other cried out to save his life, and offered great sums of money to the boatman and him to save his life. But no proffers

8*

would be heard, nor mercy would they extend, but as cruel murderers without pity slew the other also, and bound them face to face, and so threw them into the Thames in the foresaid place, where they were long after before they were found. But immediately the harlot Wolfe's wife went to the strangers' chambers, and took from thence so much as she could come by. And at last she and her husband (as they deserved) were apprehended, arraigned, and hanged at the aforesaid Turning Tree.'

Floating on the Thames] QB: *Temmes*.

Though I sit as low as Saint Faith's] Compare Beaumont and Fletcher, The Knight of the Burning Pestle V, 1:
 Since my true love is gone, I never more
 Whilst I do live upon the sky will pore:
 But in the dark will wear out my shoe-soles
 In passion, in Saint Faith's church under Paul's.

Exit] Both Qs: *Exit Constable*.

God ye good night &c.] Compare Romeo and Juliet II, 4: *Nurse: God ye good morrow, gentlemen. Mer.: God ye good den, fair gentlewoman.* — Instead of '*twenty, sir*' QD reads: *Twentysir*. Compare Merry Wives II, 1: *Good even and twenty, good Master Page*.

P. 27.

Every senseless watchman] QB: *sensible*. (See Corrigenda.)

I'faith] QD: *faith*.

He is a cobbler] Both Qs: *he was a cobbler*.

I see a man i' th' moon &c.] Printed as prose in both Qs.

By my fekins] Both Qs: *fekings*. Compare The Winter's Tale I, 2: *I'fecks*.

It behoves us all to be so] Both Qs: *I behoves*. QD omits '*to*'.

P. 28.

Enter King and Compton with bills on their backs] Both Qs: *on his backe*. — The germ of this fictitious episode where the king after the fashion of the Caliph Haroun and under the sonorous title of the Great Stag of Baydon walks about disguised, may perhaps be found in Holinshed, who on p. 806b relates: 'On midsummer night the king came priuilie into Cheape in one of the cotes of his gard,'

NOTES.

Soft, yonder's a light] The article is not in the Qs.

You have been at noddy] See Dyce's Glossary and Nares s. Noddy.

I am a court-card] QB: *coat-card*.

About a little business &c.] We should read: *About a little business I've in hand*.

Fond heedless men] QD: *needless*.

In highest state affairs] Both Qs: *in high state affairs*.

P. 29.

For making statutes] 'For' has been added in order to restore the metre.

There's some suspicion] QB: *suspection*.

But mumbudget] Compare Nares, Dyce's Glossary s. Mum, and the editors on The Merry Wives V, 2.

[Aside] This stage-direction is not in the Qs.

What the devil art thou?] Both Qs: *What a devil &c.*

And not budge] Both Qs: *booge*.

P. 31.

I am pleased, sir] 'Sir' is only in QD.

Goodman Prichall] Both Qs: *Sprichall*.

I'll set you] In QD '*Ile*' belongs to the foregoing page.

And if a constable &c.] We should read: *And if no constable be present by*.

P. 32.

Tell us some tidings] QD: *tiding*.

Exeunt] Both Qs: *Exit*.

P. 33.

Two gulls are light into my hands] Perhaps: 'are lighted'. See however Mr. Abbott's Shakespearian Grammar 342.

And in this wretched counters] Thus both Qs.

And without that, nought &c.] A trochaic verse. We should read: *And there's without that &c.*

A poor gentleman] The metre seems to require the expunction of the epithet '*poor*'.

P. 34.

And so is quite undone] See Mr. Abbott's Shakespearian Grammar 399.

Thus kings and lords, I see] This would be a regular blank verse but for the superfluous interpolation of the words '*and lords*'.

Where's this bully Grig] Grig, or rather Greg, may be taken for an abbreviation of Gregory, and '*bully Greg*' may probably mean the same person as '*Turk Gregory*' in 1 K. Henry IV, V, 3.

Shall I teach thee some wit &c.] Printed as verse as far as: '*How lik'st thou this, my bully?*'

Why I meet thee here] Both Qs: *met thee here.*

There was watch laid] QD: *there's watch laid.*

Forget our chief guest] For the omission of '*I*' see Shakespearian Grammar 400. K. Richard III, III, 4: *Marry, and will, my lord, with all my heart.*

P. 35.

No right cavalier] Both Qs: *not right cavalier.*

To first Prisoner] This stage-direction is not in the Qs.

We were more familiar] Thus both Qs, against the metre; I think, we should read: *we have been more familiar.*

You see, policies &c.] The metre might be restored by inserting '*now*' after '*see*'.

Away with him] Both Qs: *Goe away with him.*

Exeunt Porter &c.] Both Qs: *Exit &c.*

'*Swoons, I shall &c.*] Perhaps either: '*Swoons, I shall go to Tyburn &c.* or: '*Swoons, now I shall to Tyburn &c.* — Black Will speaks in verse once more, infrà: *Fore God, ye broke my head most gallantly.*

P. 36.

The gentlemen &c.] Both Qs, printing this and the following line as prose, read '*Gentlemen*' — without the article.

Drink to King Harry's health] The preposition '*to*' spoils the metre.

Though ye misliked my play] QD: *mislike*.

The vulgar hot-shots] Compare The Puritan I, 2: *Where be your muskets, calivers, and hot-shots?*

As e'er cannon against &c.] QB: *as ere carried against &c.*

P. 37.

I thank you for your lodging] QB: *for our lodging*.

Discharge the officers] Both Qs: *offices*.

Exit keeper] QB: *Ex.* QD: *Exit.* — both without naming the person that is to leave the stage.

Most true, my lord] Qy: *'Tis most true, my lord?*

Alas, poor Mary, so soon] Qy: *art so soon?*

We must then prepare] '*Then*' ought to be expunged, or placed at the end of the line instead of '*too*'.

Dreadless of the proudest] In order to restore the metre we should read: *that's dreadless &c.*

I shall, my sovereign] '*Sovereign*' is to be pronounced as a trisyllable. Compare Love's Labour's Lost III, 1: *The anointed sovereign of sighs and groans*. K. Richard II, II, 2: *The one's my sovereign, whom both my oath &c.*

The lady Katherine Parr] Both Qs here as well as on p. 39: *Parry*. Hall and Holinshed write *Par*.

And Anne of Clere] Both Qs: *Cleaue*.

Exeunt] Both Qs: *Exit*.

P. 38.

Mislikes his praises, but] Both Qs end this line with '*praises*' and begin the following with '*But*'. The metre, however, as well as the rhyme, point out the correct reading.

Enter the cardinal &c.] From the following speeches of Will Summers (p. 38: *I heard say your lordship had made two new lords here*) and of Wolsey (p. 39: *But, bishops, we'll to court immediately;* ibid.. *You two are tutors to the princess Mary*) it appears that Wolsey is attended by two bishops. Compare the king's question at p. 45: *What say ye, reverend lords*, which is replied to by Bonner and Gardiner. Gardiner, therefore, is the other bishop who enters together with Wolsey and Bonner.

The fool shall ride you] QD: *shall aide you.*—Compare Chapman's Tragedy of Alphonsus ed. Elze (Leipzig, 1867) p. 78: *Have with thee, marshall, the fool rides thee.*—Timon of Athens II, 1: *Isid. Serv. There's the fool hangs on your back already. Apem. No, thou standst single, thou'rt not on him yet.*

P. 39.

The bells hang high &c.] In both Qs these verses are printed as prose.

P. 40.

Exeunt; manent &c.] In the Qs this stage-direction runs as follows: '*Manet Will and Patch. Exeunt omnes.*'

There's no fool to the wilful still] This is the reading of QB. QD: *there's no fool to thee, Will. fool still.*—Perhaps these words should be divided between the two fools, thus: *Patch. There's no fool to thee, Will. Will. Fool still. What shall we do, cousin?* But even such an arrangement seems not to clear away all difficulty.

Exeunt] Both Qs: *Exit*.

By us thus dignified] After this line a verse or two seem to be wanting.

P. 41.

Doctor Tye] Christopher Tye, doctor of music, was musical preceptor to the children of Henry VIII. and organist of the royal chapel, for which he wrote a great many sacred compositions. As mentioned below, he set to music a portion of '*The Actes of the Apostles, translated into Englyshe metre*', which was printed in 1553. Anthony Wood describes him as 'a peevish, humorsome man, especially in his latter days'. Doctor Tye died about 1580.

Provide civil oranges enough] Civil, of course, for Seville. Compare Much Ado II, 1: *But civil count, civil as an orange, and something of that jealous complexion.* See Dyce's Gl. s. Civil. The pun contained in '*lemon*' needs no explanation.

Unhappily slain a man] Thus QD. QB: *unhappily hath slain a man*.

Thou killedst the t'other] See Shakespearian Grammar 12.

P. 42.

What, a Lutheran] Both Qs: *what a Lutheran?*

Enquire for Rokesby] The Qs write '*Rookesby*'.

There's shrewder heads] QB: *shrouder;* QD: *shrowder*.

Thus to extirp] This curious — if not corrupted — expression occurs again on p. 55: *She did extirp against his holiness*.

Great quarrellers &c.] Printed as prose.

P. 43.

Your poor servant &c.] '*Poor*' may be added to the list of monosyllables pronounced as dissyllables given in Mr. Abbott's Shakespearian Grammar 480. — Instead of '*is so called*' QB reads '*so called*'.

It likes not our majesty] Perhaps either: '*T likes &c*. or: *It liketh not &c*.

For that we know] Compare p. 50: *I have thought of that ye read last night*. See Shakespearian Grammar 244.

Surely some envious man] Both Qs: *Sure &c*.

Villain, those that guard me &c.] A line without metre, unless '*Villain*' be read as a monosyllable. The same holds good in the next line but one, where '*Under*' is used as a monosyllable and '*march*' as a dissyllable. '*Purgatory*' in the verse then following is a trisyllable; '*God's*' (*God's dear lady*) three lines further on, a dissyllable. See Mr. Abbott's Shakespearian Grammar 464, 477, 478, 482.

P. 44.

Enter a Messenger] Both Qs print this stage-direction after the words: *My royal lord,* which moreover they erroneously assign to Rokesby instead of the messenger.

Ha! pardon thee &c.] In the Qs this speech of the king is printed as prose. In order to restore the metre I have only added '*all*' before the words: *the world should purchase it*.

Hinderance] Thus QB. QD: *hindrance*.

Exit Rokesby] The name has been added.

Is for my servants meant] Both Qs: *Is meant for my servants*.

That brings us news] Both Qs: *that brings this news*.

Duke Brandon, good my liege] '*Good*' is not in the Qs.

P. 45.

'Tis said, my liege, &c.] Both Qs: *'Tis said they were married at Dover, my liege.*

Enter Brandon and Lady Mary] '*Lady*' is not in the Qs.

Off with his head!] In Cavendish's Life of Wolsey (ed. Singer, I, 168 seq.) it is reported that Henry was incensed at the marriage and that Brandon stood in danger of losing his head, and was only saved by the interposition of Wolsey. — It will be observed that the famous order of K. Richard III. respecting the Duke of Buckingham, in Colley Cibber's alteration of the play, is couched in the same words.

Nay, you have taken leave] This and the following line are printed as prose.

Will scarce save yourself] We should read: *scarce will save yourself.*

That you broke a lance] '*That*' is not in the Qs.

Q. Kath. O good my lord] Both Qs: *O my lord.*

What say ye, reverend lords] '*Reverend*' is an addition of mine again. See note on p. 38: *Enter the cardinal &c.*

King. He deserves it then? &c.] The metre might thus be restored: *He then deserves it? — So he does, my liege.*

I do love you both] Qs: *I love you both.*

Now, tell on, Brandon] Qs: *And tell on, Brandon.*

P. 46.

And the king shall meet] The article is not in the Qs.

I'll go and call] Qs: *I'll go call.* Or should we read: *I will go call?*

Go, bear this youngster &c.] In the Qs this speech, which undoubtedly belongs to Cranmer, is given to young Browne himself.

The prince, sir, will not learn] Both Qs: *The prince will not learn, sir.*

P. 47.

Exeunt and Re-enter young Browne with Will Summers] Both these stage-directions have been added.

The mote in thine eye] See the notes on the well-known passage in Hamlet I, 1.

Yet, in truth] Both Qs: *yet, in troth*.

P. 48.

Though Ramus himself] Petrus Ramus, the celebrated author of '*Aristotelicæ Animadversiones*', '*Institutiones Dialecticæ*', and numerous other works, which in their time were highly popular not only in France, but also in England and Germany. He embraced protestantism and perished in the massacre of St. Bartholomew.

Well, proba] Both Qs: *well, probe*.

Enter the King] In the Qs this stage-direction precedes the speech of the young marquess.

P. 49.

Donzel del Phebo] Both Qs: *Donsal delphebus*. The celebrated hero in the Mirrour of Knighthood is meant.

King. Confirm it &c.] In both Qs this speech is printed as prose.

Thou'st honoured me] Qs: *thou hast &c.*

To types of dignity] QD: *or dignity*.

Under forma pauperis] Both Qs: *papris*.

P. 50.

I thank your majesty &c.] In the Qs the first line of this speech ends after '*majesty*'.

Lords and gentlemen, give leave] '*And*' is not in the Qs.

Omne animal est aut homo, aut bestia] The instruction here given to the prince by Cranmer is a somewhat stale mimicry of the dialectics of Petrus Ramus, in whose '*Aristotelicæ Animadversiones*' (ed. Freigius, Basil. 1575) we read amongst others the following syllogisms, p. 171: 'Omnis homo necessario est rationalis: quiduis currens homo est: soli enim currunt homines, vt Aristoteles in pari enunciati soluti exemplo sumit omne auimal moveri. Ergo omnia currentia necessario rationalia sunt.' And on p. 184: 'Omnis homo, omnisque bellua sentit: omne animal homo est, belluave: omne igitur animal sentit.' This mockery does not only show, how far Ramism was spread in England, but it also implies, that the blame cast on Ramus by Bacon (*De interpretatione naturæ*) as 'ignorantiæ latibulum, perniciosissima literarum tinea, compendiorum pater, qui cum methodi suæ et

9*

compendii vinclis res torqueat et premat, res quidem, si qua fuit, elabitur protinus et exsilit; ipse vero aridas et desertissimas nugas stringit' — found an echo in the non-professional ranks of the public. See Hallam, Introd. Lit. Eur. II, 368.

Est rationale &c.] Both Qs: *est rationalis et irrationalis.*

P. 51.

And so all beasts] Both Qs: *and though all beasts.*

Serving instead of feet] By the expunction of '*serving*' this line might be reduced to a regular blank verse.

Dentes supremos] Both Qs: *dentes supremas.*

Cedant arma togæ] QD: *cedent.*

Prince. Well, Cranmer &c.] This speech is no doubt corrupt and mutilated. QB, to which I have here strictly adhered, entirely assigns it to the Prince as far as '*How thinks your grace*', whilst in QD the line: *God give ye truth, that you may give it me,* which manifestly belongs to the Prince, together with the four subsequent lines, is given to Cranmer.

Ye speak] In the Qs these words form part of the preceding verse.

Truly, I think none &c.] This and the following verses of this speech are differently divided in the Qs. —Instead of '*Truly, I think none*' the metre would require '*I think none, truly*'.

P. 52.

May your grace ever delight] Qy: *May your grace take e'er delight?*

P. 53.

Shall make that place] '*Make*' here seems used in the same sense as seamen use it in the phrase '*to make a port*' i. e. to reach it, to arrive at it.

Thou giv'st it perfect life &c.] '*Life*' is to be pronounced as a dissyllable, although not contained in Mr. Abbott's list, Shakespearian Grammar 484. Or should we read: *most skilful doctor?*

P. 54.

Worthy Acts and worthily &c.] This line should be given to the Prince instead of Doctort Tye.

French and Italian] Both Qs: *Italians*.

Exeunt omnes] This stage-direction is not in the Qs.

Luther has sown well] We should read: *For Luther has sown well*.

What? bishops and prelates] '*Prelátes*' may be added to Mr. Abbott's list, Shakespearian Grammar 490.

Ay, nobility temporal] Qy: *And nobles temporal?* Or: *Ay, and nobility temporal?*

Whether he will bend] '*Whether*' has been added.

P. 55.

How in presence] Qy: *How in the presence?*

But had our English cardinal] It should be: *Had but our English cardinal.—'Cardinal'* is either to be pronounced as a dissyllable, or '*once*' to be struck out.

Attend his excellence] QD: *excellency*.

Set forward, gentlemen] Both Qs: *Gentlemen, set forward*.

It seems the king is coming] Both Qs: *the queen is coming*.

Bran. My liege] If we were to read: '*Here, my liege*', the three speeches combined would constitute a regular blank verse.

P. 56.

Their friendship must advance &c.] The true reading most probably is: *Their friendship must his dignity advance*, as there can be little doubt, that the author has chosen the unusual word '*governance*' for the sake of the rhyme.

I tell ye, lords &c.] This and the following verses spoken by the king are printed as prose in the Qs. No changes have been made except the addition of '*I*' before '*pray God, there be not*', and '*I do not like this difference*' instead of '*I like not this difference*'.

As half the province] Qy: *And half the province?* In the name '*Helvetia*' a corruption may be suspected; perhaps '*Westphalia*'.

P. 57.

Methinks, 'twere well &c.] There is so close a resemblance between the following scenes and the relation given of Queen

Katherine Parr's troubles by Lord Herbert of Cherbury in his Life and Reign of K. Henry VIII. (1649, p. 560 seq.) that the latter must no doubt be considered as the poet's source. Holinshed (in his second edition) makes no other mention of Katherine Parr, than that she married the king and was proclaimed queen. The only part of this episode, as represented by Rowley, which is not borne out by historical evidence, is the share which he ascribes to the Prince of Wales, at that time scarcely nine years of age.

The superstitions and the church &c.] Both Qs: *And superstitions against the Church of Rome.*

Most unlawful] Perhaps: *'Tis most unlawful;* or: *Nay, most unlawful.*

Well said, Kate] In the Qs this speech is printed as prose. The only alteration made is the expunction of *'there'* after the words: *Avoid the presence.*

I am a weak scholar &c.] This and the two following verses might be thus reduced to regular metre:
   I am a weak scholar, but on condition
   That nor your highness, nor these reverend lords,
   Will take exceptions at my woman's wit &c.

Tell me, why would] Both Qs: *Pray tell me &c.* Or are we to read: *Pray, tell me, why you'ld make &c.?*

These are that sect] Both Qs: *that sects.*

'Tis true, but pray ye &c.] The metre requires the addition of *'my lord'* after *"tis true'.*

P. 58.

Were it to any one] *'One'* should be struck out.

Pray tell the king then] Qy: *Pray tell his highness then &c.?*

Of Cranmer, Ridley &c.] *'Of'* has been added.

As by their articles is evident] Both Qs: *are evident.*

Ah, sirrah, we have women doctors] Both Qs here and on p. 77: *a sirra.* 'Sirrah' was not unfrequently used as an address to a woman. See Dyce's Glossary s. Sirrah.

It breed no further detriment] QD: *farther.*

King. Ha! Take heed what you do say, Gardiner!] Qy: *Ha! Gardiner, take heed what you do say?*

P. 59.

Arose in arms] Both Qs: *arise in arms*.

We pardon what ye speak, resolve us speedily] Qy: *resolve us quickly?*

P. 60.

Reads the letter] This stage-direction has been added.

Lord Bishops] See Mr. Abbott's Shakespearian Grammar 430.

When he thought to find John Baptist &c.] This quotation, like the letters from the princesses Mary and Elizabeth, seems to be due to the author's invention, at least I have not been able to trace it in the letters and writings of Dr. Luther against K. Henry VIII. Luther's reply (*Contra Henricum Regem Angliæ*) to the king's first pamphlet (1522) was published in the same year at Wittenberg, both in the Latin original and in a German translation, the latter being still more violent and abusive than the former. In January 1523 the king complained to the elector and to Duke George and from the latter received an answer (May 1523) strongly disapproving of Luther's vehemence. In September 1525 Luther asked the king's pardon for his rudeness—'*by fawning speeches*', as our author expresses it. The controversy, however, was renewed and continued till 1527, in which year Luther published his pamphlet '*Auf des Königs von England Lästerschrift Titel*' and thereby gave offence even to some of his own friends. See *Dr. M. Luther's Briefe, Sendschreiben und Bedenken herausgeg. von de Wette (Berlin, 1827.)*

False Luther knows] QB: *knaues*; QD: *knaves*.

The greatest Lutherin] Qy: *Lutheran?*—if a rhyme be not intended with the preceding line: *plead for him.*

P. 61.

From your grace's sister &c.] Qy: '*Tis from your grace's sister, lady Mary?*

Enter second Servant] This and the following stage-direction (*Exeunt Cranmer and Tye*) are not in the Qs.

Be intermissers] This unheard-of expression may be a corruption of '*intercessors*', it is however in both Qs.

P. 62.

My contemplation's cures &c.] Perhaps '*my contemplation's cares*' and in the following line '*And on thy virtues*' &c.

Tye. Ay, my good lord, &c.] This line as well as the verse: *Here comes Sir William Compton &c.*, both of which are given to Tye in the Qs, should be assigned to Cranmer. Tye has left the presence together with Cranmer by the prince's order and only comes back to announce the queen (on p. 63).

Health to your excellence] QD: *excellency.*

P. 63.

Cranmer banished the court?] Qy: *What! Cranmer banished &c.?*

So help me heaven] QD: *so help ye heaven.*

Exit Compton] Both this stage-direction and the exit of Tye are not in the Qs; the entrances of Tye and of the queen are marked in wrong places.

Avoid the presence then] The metre requires the omission of '*then*'.

P. 64.

Kate Parr still] In this very passage, where the metre seems to require the form '*Parry*', both Qs read '*Parre*'.

Which I, in love and duty] Both Qs omit '*I*'.

P. 65.

Exeunt] Both Qs: *Exit.*

Came so luckily] Both Qs: *came and so luckily.*

P. 66.

From his side we'll hale her] Thus both Qs; the same word on p. 71 is written '*hawle*'.

Guard, watch the doors] '*Doors*' is again to be read as a dissyllable.

Now in his old age] Both Qs: *in this old age.*

P. 67.

Say ye sir, ha!] Qy: *save ye sir, ha?*

P. 68.

If it hath traitorous blood] QB: *have.* QD: *traytors.*

Our faithful subiects testify] Both Qs: *can testifie.*

Which, join'd with other complots, show itself] Thus both Qs.
Thought of ill against your majesty] Qy: *your grace,* or: *your highness?*

P. 69.

Take my ring] Both Qs: *here take my ring.*
And the English court] Qy: *and our court?*
Exit Compton] This stage-direction has been added.
Enter Bonner and Gardiner &c.] According to Herbert it was not Bishop Gardiner (assisted by Bonner), but lord chancellor Wriothesley, who attempted to arrest the queen by the side of the king, with whom she was walking in the garden.

P. 70.

See yonder she is talking &c.] Both Qs: *she's.*—By reading 'with his grace' instead of 'with his majesty' we might reduce the line to a regular blank verse.
Now, wherefore come you?] I think we should add 'here'· *Now, wherefore come you here?*
Of your own inventions] Qy: *invention?*
Both my hands] QB: *hand.* This speech is partly printed as prose.

P. 71.

I have forgot it] Both Qs against the metre: *forgotten.*
Attend the prince there] 'There' should be struck out.
Hath not your tedious journey] QB: *our tedious journey.*
While the cardinal come] See Shakespearian Grammar 137.

P. 72.

Six tuns filled with plate] QB: *six times.*
You wrong the cardinal] The poet no doubt wrote: *you do wrong &c.*
I pray you, set on &c.] The metre requires the omission of 'I'.
Great Maximilian &c.] 'Whilest the Frenchmen, says Holinshed (1587, p. 821) were thus prepared to come with vittels to Terwine (i. e. Therouanne, south of St. Omer), the emperour Maximilian came from Aire to the kings campe before Terwine the twelfe of August (1513), wearing a cross of Saint George as the kings souldier and receiuing of him salarie for seruice.' Lord Herbert of Cherbury in his Life and Reign of K. Henry VIII.

(ed. 1649, p. 38) adds, that Maximilian's pay is said to have been a hundred crowns *per diem*.

P. 73.

'Tis no matter, Kate] ''Tis' should be omitted.

A High Court Legatine] Holinshed (p. 845) says: 'This man (viz. John Clarke, who had attended Campeius to Rome, as ambassador from the king) obteined for the cardinall, authoritie to dispense with all men for offenses committed against the spirituall lawes, which part of his power legantine was verie profitable and gainefull. For then he set up a court, and called it the court of the legat: in the which he prooued testaments, and heard causes, to the great hinderance of all the bishops of this realme. He visited bishops, and all the cleargie exempt and not exempt, and vnder colour of reformation he got much treasure. For thorough bribes and rewards, notorious offendors were dispensed with, so that nothing was reformed, but came to more mischeefe.'

Which he belike hath hid] QD: *which belike he hath hid.*

We thank your pains &c.] QD: *we thank you for your pains.* Compare All's Well that Ends Well V, 1: *But rather make you thank your pains for it.* — Or should we read: *We thank you for your pains, lord cardinal?*

And much our longing eyes] QD: *loving eyes.*

But see, lord cardinal] Both Qs: *lord Admirall.*

P. 75.

Where raging Boreas flies] QB: *styes.*

And now must chide you] Qy: *but we now must chide you?*

P. 76.

Hateful impudence] Both Qs: *impudency.*

Secret conveyance &c.] Taken from Holinshed (p. 912): 'Item, he without the kings assent carried the kings great seal with him into Flanders, when he was sent ambassador to the pope.'

There keep you &c.] The correct reading probably is: *There keep, until you further hear from us.*

P. 78.

And girt in complete steel] Compare Hamlet I, 4:
  That thou, dead corse, again in complete steel
  Revisit'st us.

And sit installed therewith at Windsor Castle] 'At Windsor, relates Holinshed (p. 873), they (viz. the emperor and the king) taried a whole weeke and more, where on Corpus Christi daie (1523), the emperour ware his mantell of the Garter, and sate in his owne stall.'

P. 79.

Wrestle, shoot, &c.] Qy: *Shoot, wrestle &c.*?

WHILE these sheets have been going through the press, another suggestion has offered itself to me respecting the relation in which Rowley's piece may have stood to Shakespeare's K. Henry VIII., viz. that it may have been an opposition-play set up against the latter by a rival company. Supposing K. Henry VIII. to have been produced in 1603, '*When you see me, you know me*' may have been written and brought on the stage in 1604. All the coincidences with Shakespeare, the passages which refer to the Taming of the Shrew and to the Merchant of Venice included, would then turn out simply to be imitations by Rowley. In a word, the relation between Rowley's piece and Henry VIII. would then be the very same, as that between Chettle's Hoffman and Hamlet, according to the elaborate and ingenious disquisition of my learned friend Professor Dr. Delius in the *Jahrbuch der Deutschen Shakespeare-Gesellschaft* IX, 166—194. This suggestion, however apt to clear away all difficulties, will of course find no favour with those critics who persist in ascribing Henry VIII. to the year 1613; but I am afraid that the more impartially it be weighed, the stronger an argument it may prove against them. After all Shakespeare's Henry VIII. was only revived in 1613 and the revival and republication of '*When you see me, you know me*' followed close after it. That the Prologue and Epilogue of Henry VIII. were only added in 1613 and hint most distinctly at the rival play, seems to admit of no doubt.

ADDENDA AND CORRIGENDA.

P. XIII. Instead of: *there is 'no sallet in the lines'* read: *there are 'no sallets in the lines'*.

P. 8. Instead of: *all swines flesh &c.* read: *all swine's flesh &c.*

P. 27. Some lines have been omitted. Read:
First Watch. How say ye? By my faith, neighbour Prichall, ye speak to the purpose: for indeed, neighbours, every senseless watchman is to seek the best reformation to his own destruction.
Sec. Watch. But what think ye, neighbours, if every man. take a nap now i' th' forehand o' th' night and go to bed afterward?
Prich. That were not amiss neither &c.

P. 84. The second edition of Holinshed here and elsewhere has been assigned to the year 1586 instead of 1587. It was printed in 1586, but published only in January 1587.

P. 91. To the notes on p. 21 the following is to be added:
When thou comest close to him, cry Bo!] This seems to have been a favourite trick with all domestic fools. Compare *Wily Beguiled* (Hawkins, The Origin of the English Drama III, 319): I'll rather put on my flashing red nose, and my flaming face, and come wrapped in a calf's-skin, and cry, *bo, bo*: I'll fray the scholar, I warrant thee.

www.ingramcontent.com/pod-product-compliance
Lightning Source LLC
Chambersburg PA
CBHW022132160426
43197CB00009B/1256